How to Spot the Spirit's Work in Your Life

Seek His Gifts and Fruit

David S. Luecke

WESTBOW
P R E S S®
A DIVISION OF THOMAS NELSON
& ZONDERVAN

WestBow Press books may be ordered through booksellers or by contacting:

WestBow Press
A Division of Thomas Nelson & Zondervan
1663 Liberty Drive
Bloomington, IN 47403
www.westbowpress.com
1 (866) 928-1240

ISBN: 978-1-5127-5274-8 (sc)
ISBN: 978-1-5127-5272-4 (e)

Library of Congress Control Number: 2016914607

Print information available on the last page.

WestBow Press rev. date: 09/14/2016

Contents

Part 1: Naming the Issues

Discussion 1

The Spirit Is the Key to Thriving in Christ

Believers who raise their awareness of the Holy Spirit, practice GROWTH in the Spirit and share their experiences will find their Christian life becomes more exciting and fulfilling. Pastors who teach Spirit awareness and GROWTH practices will see their congregation become more stimulating, healthy and attractive.

To thrive "spiritually" addresses a dimension more or higher than prospering materially. Christians know God is the key to thriving spiritually. But we are too often unclear about how this happens. The meaning of "spiritual" can remain vague.

Biblically the definition is straightforward: *spiritual* is associated with the work of the Spirit. Usually called just "the Spirit," sometimes he is named the "Holy Spirit." He is also named the "Spirit from God" or the "Spirit from Christ."[1]

What the Spirit did throughout Bible history can be made complicated. Keep it simple by focusing only on what the Spirit does for believers here and now. Paul prayed that "the Father may strengthen you with power through his Spirit in your inner being, so that Christ may dwell in your hearts through faith."[2] "God poured out his love into our hearts through the Holy Spirit, whom he has given us."[3] The *Holy* Spirit is a description of the Spirit of holiness, and "the Spirit of holiness was declared with power to be the Son of God."[4]

1

The Spirit that the Father and the Son send in turn gives believers special gifts. Paul considered these gifts of the Spirit to be the key to thriving spiritually as people of God.

What are those special gifts of the Spirit? He described some as the greater gifts of love, faith, and hope. These are part of his larger listing of the product or fruit of the Spirit's work in hearts of God's people: love, joy, peace, patience, kindness, gentleness, faithfulness, goodness, and self-control. To thrive spiritually means to discover and experience growth in such inner qualities worked by the Spirit. He extends into our lives "the riches of God's kindness, tolerance and patience."[5]

The other kind of gifts or manifestations of the Spirit, according to Paul, are believers specially motivated to serve the common good of Christ's people according to their differing talents and interests. Churches that benefit from such Spirit-driven energy of Spirit-shaped believers will thrive, regardless of their numeric size.

When we focus on Christ's Spirit, we can learn to expect the Spirit to enrich us with his gifts. Those gifts are an extension of God's basic grace, by which he freely gives believers his favor and salvation without the need to earn them. By grace God reaches out to draw us to the Savior. By grace the Spirit moves to enrich our inner lives with his fruit and special energy.

This focus on the gifts of the Spirit can for traditional churches amount to a new approach to understanding and leading church life today. It isn't really new, because Paul explained and used it in his church leadership. But it needs to be renewed among traditional churches that proudly maintain their heritage of church and ministry practiced over the centuries since the Reformation. For all practical purposes, the ministries of Episcopalians, Lutherans, and Calvinists (those who are Presbyterian and Reformed and many Baptists) have overlooked the active work of the Spirit in changing lives today. Certainly the Spirit has always been part of the *Tr*initarian formula of Father, Son, and Spirit. But the special gifts of the Spirit usually aren't part of our formula for doing ministry among those we encounter today. We focus on God the Father and God the Son—a *bi*nitarian emphasis.

While Christ's Spirit has always been active among believers, he can bring more growth to our faith lives when we learn to recognize how he works and pray for his special influence. We can become more aware of the Spirit at work in and around us. Our personal challenge is to put ourselves where the Spirit can most effectively change us. The ministry challenge is to be fully *Tri*nitarian in featuring all God does for his people.

This book is about those challenges. It aims to be very practical by offering six practices that put us more directly in the pathway the Spirit can use best for our individual temperaments. These practices are the following, presented in the acronym GROWTH:

1. *Go* to God in worship and prayer.
2. *Receive* God's word for you.
3. *Own* your self-denial.
4. Give *witness* to your experiences.
5. *Trust* God in a new venture.
6. *Humble* yourself before God.

Recognize these as GROWTH practices.

A while ago a committee at my church spent a year designing a visual logo to summarize what we are about. They chose three words: *connect, belong,* and *thrive.* Our leaders will aim to effectively *connect* with people beyond our church, to purposefully help them *belong* to this fellowship, and to deliberately provide resources so they can *thrive* in their relationships with God.

To thrive in one's Christian faith is an exciting goal and was clearly a high priority for the committee. Ways to better connect and belong are projects we can figure out and do with planning and hard work. How do we help believers thrive? This is a tougher challenge. What does a thriving faith look like? This book explores in depth what is involved in thriving spiritually.

To be sure, the basic resource to thrive spiritually is God's word. We can and should be continually asking how we can more present biblical truths in ways participants find most relevant to their personal lives. Ultimately, such personal perception and application are enlightenment the Spirit grants. While we can plant and water seeds, the Spirit from God makes them grow into a thriving faith life.

So an extension of the challenge to present God's word creatively is to develop additional ways to help believers put themselves where the Spirit can most effectively grow them in a flourishing life with God. The GROWTH practices are one attempt. Believers who do these six practices at least once a week will put themselves into situations that stretch their faith and cause them to reflect on what is happening. Sharing or giving witness to their experiences will help develop a church culture that is more receptive to the Spirit's ongoing work in their midst.

Traditional mainline churches would do well to accept the challenge to refocus attention on the Spirit's gifts because so many of those congregations no longer appear to be thriving, at least by outward appearances. Decline in members and dollars has been under way over the last forty-five years, increasingly so since 2000. More explicit emphasis on the Spirit didn't seem necessary over the centuries and up until this general decline. Unheralded, the Spirit was getting his work done, and most traditional congregations were thriving. But their formula for binitarian ministry focused on the Father and the Son is no longer so effective.

While traditional churches have been declining, a new kind of Christianity has flourished among believers who highlight and celebrate the gifts of the Spirit. They go by the name Pentecostal. Most feature the gift of speaking in strange tongues, as happened on the first Pentecost when the Spirit moved mightily in Jerusalem and brought thousands to faith in the crucified and resurrected Jesus Christ. In recent decades, the Spirit has moved mightily, especially in other parts of the world. Almost all of that growth is happening among believers with heightened experiences of the gifts of the Spirit. Their approach isn't a traditional one to understanding and living the Christian faith.

Traditional Protestant Christians come from a heritage that features a very rational understanding and application of the biblical word of God. That heritage makes us resistant to irrational experiences. But the Spirit wants to give many other gifts that would be appreciated in any congregation. These would especially be fruit such as love, joy, peace, and patience. Consider those gifts to be Spirit-generated feelings and not just virtues to be pursued on our own. Naming and sharing experiences of the Spirit have great value in sharing the faith. Reclaiming Paul's emphasis on the Spirit's gifts can bring renewal to traditional Protestant churches.

The Joy-Giving Jesus Christ

Many Christians over time have focused on Jesus as reflected in the emphases of Matthew's Gospel account. This is the Jesus of judgment, who set the high standards in his Sermon on the Mount and who will separate the sheep from the goats at the final judgement. Matthew confused us by giving the kingdom of God the name "kingdom of heaven," which we too easily think of as coming later but is something we need to prepare for now. That demanding Jesus dominated the thoughts of Christians and their leaders for most of church history, along with issues of how to be faithful and pass the coming judgment.

The life of Jesus certainly remains an important guide for us so we can live more God-pleasing lives. But exhortations to live like Christ often come with phrases like "you must do" this or that. Usually meant as a motivator, this language tends to slip into what Christians "have to do" and places the emphasis on our actions rather than on the good news of actions God took and still takes today. This view of a demanding Jesus is the easiest way to fit him into categories we can work with. But concentrating on the rules and "shoulds" for Christian beliefs and practice can often make life in Christ seem like a grim task. If we don't thrive in Christlike behavior, we too readily conclude that we just have to work harder.

The evangelist John best offers us glimpses of the softer, joy-giving side of Jesus Christ. This is the Good Shepherd who came that his followers may have the abundant life now, life that is overflowing.[6] John recorded that Jesus, in the image of himself as the vine and us as the branches embedded in him, expects his joy and ours to be completed.[7] Those branches will bear much fruit, a result Paul later identified as fruit of the Spirit. Preparing his disciples for his ascension, Jesus stressed that, after grieving his departure, they would experience a full measure of "my joy."[8] This is the Jesus of peace and joy and life overflowing, with the real blessings that are basic to good living.

It is John, too, who recorded Jesus's expectation that the truest worship of the Father is done in spirit and truth.[9] Such worship we can try to accomplish by featuring biblical truths. But it is very hard to turn head-based worship in truth into a heartfelt response in the Spirit. It takes the Spirit to make spirited worship possible.

In addition to John, Luke, in his account of Jesus's ministry, emphasized the joy and celebration he brings. Luke recalled the most parables of grace—stories of people getting what they don't deserve and not getting what, by ordinary thinking, they do deserve. The only possible response to God's grace and mercy is joy and thanksgiving. Luke specialized in party parables, such as the one about the father who welcomed home his lost son with a feast of celebration.[10] He wanted us to understand that God's kingdom brings lots of joy to celebrate.

Luke also wanted us to understand that we can enjoy the good life God offers now, not only later. He did this with his special emphasis on the healings Jesus did. The significance of such healings got lost to readers who were unfamiliar with the original Gospel accounts. The verb used for "to heal" is the same as the verb for "to save," which we usually take to mean being saved for the eternal feast. But it also means to be saved for health and joy in this life. We can rightfully talk about the present salvation Jesus offers.

In Matthew's account of Jesus's words to his disciples just before his ascent, Jesus commanded them to go and make more disciples. Luke added that Jesus first said, "Wait in the city until you have been clothed with power from on high." The Spirit empowered the growth of Christianity, not just the hard work of his disciples.

Paul's Emphasis on the Spirit

Most of the reading of Paul over the centuries focuses on Christ's meaning for our lives today. Typically overlooked, though, is his explanation of how the Spirit empowers such Christlike living. Paul referred to being "in Christ" eighty-one times in his letters. In contrast, there are the 143 passages where he explained that living in Christ is made possible for us by the Spirit. The conventional view is that justification by faith is the core of Paul's theology. Eminent scholars today, however, suggest that the work of the Spirit is even more central."[11]

The issues I want to address for Christians and their churches today can best be understood by recognizing that in Paul's thinking Christ today and the Spirit's presence today are really two sides of the same coin. The coin is God at work among his people. Paul sometimes reflected in a one-side manner and sometimes in the other-side manner interchangeably. This key insight provides a new perspective on energy for living the present Christian life. Instead of focusing only on the Christ side, let the Spirit side also influence ministry today.

A member of our congregation has a specialized coin ministry. Through what can be described only as an encounter with the Spirit, Kevin felt called to design, make, and distribute a coin that is about the size of a half dollar. One side has a cross symbol surrounded with the words "Mercy is not getting what we deserve." The other side shows the Spirit dove with the words "Grace is getting what we do not deserve." Giving the coin away provides an opportunity for a great Christian witness, and over one hundred thousand coins have been distributed (hiscoin@gmail.com).

Kevin's grace and mercy coin well illustrates my main point. Historic Protestant churches have focused almost exclusively on the mercy of the Christ side, mercy earned in Jesus's death and resurrection. More effective ministry can also be found by featuring the Spirit side, which emphasizes how God through the Spirit gives us what we don't deserve, including the gifts the Spirit wants to impart. The biblical word for "grace," *charis,* means a gift freely given without expectation of return. This is God's favor we don't need to earn because Jesus Christ earned it for us. The result is the big gift that changes our relationship with God. This grace is on the Spirit side of the coin because the Spirit leads us to accept this gift.

Charisma is the gift received. In Paul's vocabulary the word *charisma* identifies additional gifts we receive from the Spirit. The plural is *charismata.* He recognized these to include the fruit of the Spirit, such as love, joy, and peace, which he called the greater gifts. The other gifts of the Spirit are special motivation to do ministries for the greater good of others.

Significantly, the root word for *charis* and *charisma* is *chara,* which means "joy." God's gifts are closely tied to our reactions of joy. Put an *eu* in front, and the word becomes *eucharistia,* meaning "thankfulness." God's gifts generate such feelings.

Those gifts have always been present in one form or another among believers throughout the history of the Christian church. We can work in our own strength to achieve a life that should bring us more joy and thanksgiving. What's better is to rely on the Spirit to work into our hearts the freedom of our grace-changed, Christ-based relationship with the Father, out of which flows new Spirit-gifted motivation and relationships with others. The deepest joy and most profound thanksgiving come from flowing in the Spirit.

Communication of gospel-based living has to be kept simple, but there are two kinds of simplicity. One is on this side of complexity; the second is on the other side of complexity. The complexity is the mystery of the Trinity. Because preachers and teachers in our heritage thought they most clearly understood what God the Father and God the Son did and do, we practice ministry with the simplicity of leaving God the Spirit only vaguely in the background and out of the working equation.

But more effective ministry comes when we confront the true mystery of the Trinity, which is beyond our ability to fully comprehend and control. What God the Son did through his earthly life enables him, as the now-ascended Christ, to advocate the redemption of each believer before God the Father. Now ascended, Christ is present with each of us today through his Spirit. While we cannot control the Spirit from Christ, we can learn to better recognize how he works and how we can put ourselves on a pathway where he can best grow us into a thriving spiritual life.

Thriving and Withering Churches

Many Christian congregations today are thriving by outward appearances. Many others are withering. What is the difference? Emphasis on the work of the Spirit here and now can explain much.

Thriving Churches

Churches that emphasize experiences of the Spirit today come with many different labels. Pentecostal is the most common. In the narrow sense it refers to churches that expect members to have the experience of speaking in strange tongues. Charismatic churches emphasize all the gifts, including speaking in tongues, which isn't required. Pentecostal is often an umbrella term for any church that recognizes the gifts of the Spirit as here and now.

Consider this figure: Of the world's two billion Christians, as of 2014 one-quarter are now Pentecostal—up from only 6 percent in 1980.[12] Most of that growth is in other parts of the world.

Here in America, consider this finding: Of the sixteen

"most vibrant, spiritually alive congregations" in one study, three-fifths highlighted the Spirit, as determined by looking at their websites. Yet classical Pentecostal churches make up only one-fifth of American congregations.[13] Not all churches that highlight the Spirit are thriving. Just most.

A major explanation for such growth is that Christians who are led to recognize experiences of the Spirit in their own lives want to share those experiences. They are excited about what is happening to them.

Withering Churches

Among Protestants in America, most withering churches are found among the mainline church bodies that enjoyed socially privileged status in their five hundred years of history since the Reformation. They maintained their special status and the loyalty of their members in the America well into the twentieth century. They were formed when the key question of the Reformation was how to be certain of salvation. Their answer was reliance on the truths presented in God's written word. Martin Luther and John Calvin were highly educated and insisted on rational explanations based on the scriptures. Their appeal was to Christian leaders who valued the printed word

Another common value of these now-withering churches is the assumption that God is no longer supernaturally involved in natural events. Calvin said most clearly that the age of miracles ended with the New Testament. A major part of that heritage is not to expect experiences of the Spirit here and now that cannot be explained rationally. This position leaves little room for a role of the Spirit that actively changes lives today.

Today's Protestant churches are spread out over a range from being highly word oriented on one end and highly Spirit oriented on the other. To repeat the simple observation offered earlier, the highly word-oriented churches tend to be withering, while the highly Spirit-oriented churches tend to be thriving.

Are the withering church bodies destined to continue their decline? Not necessarily. They can renew Paul's emphasis on the Spirit at work in believers here and now. They can learn to name and share experiences of the gifts of the Spirit in the lives of their members. They can become more purposeful in naming and sharing exciting spiritual experiences.

Irrational speaking in tongues will never be promoted in highly rational, word-oriented churches. But all Christians and their churches would welcome the rest of the Spirit's gifts. Focusing on *Christ's* Spirit is one way to distinguish this tamer approach from the *Holy* Spirit Pentecostals celebrate.

If the leading question of the Reformation was *how* to be sure of salvation, the key question in our current culture is, *why* be a Christian? A convincing answer is hard without appreciating the empowerment the Spirit gives for the more abundant life Christ offers.

Consider the possibility that old mainline churches are now withering because they have tied themselves to a world view that limits our understanding of God to what the Father and Son did in biblical times. This perspective for many can easily accommodate the modern world view that nothing exists beyond what can be sensed and measured now.

But now we are in what is commonly called the postmodern era, in which there is more openness to a reality greater than what can be explained scientifically. With it comes greater openness to extraordinary events for which there is no natural explanation—that is, miracles. With postmodernity comes a heightened desire to find purpose and meaning in life greater than accumulating material resources. Thriving spiritually has become a more compelling interest among the unchurched in our society. What a wonderful time to share a renewed interest in the apostle Paul's focus on the empowering presence of the Spirit today.

A greater emphasis on the Spirit can be fitted into classical Reformation emphases. I know that the Lutheran churches in Ethiopia and on the African island of Madagascar each now have more Lutherans than the combined total in North America. Their stories offer inspiration. Rapid growth really started when Africans themselves took on leadership of their churches. Their cultures are more oriented to the spirit world, and they are more receptive to Paul's emphasis on God the Spirit in addition to God the Father and God the Son.

Time for Traditional Churches to Reconsider the Spirit

Here are some major claims I will promote, based on Paul's theology and approach to leading churches. Traditional mainline church leaders would have brushed these assumptions to the side while their churches were dominant—well into the twentieth century. Clearly, it's time to reconsider.

- The Spirit from Christ is still alive and active in shaping believers' personal and church lives. God's interventions in the natural world and human life didn't cease after New Testament times.
- The fruit of the Spirit involves feelings, not just ways to live virtuously.
- The Spirit from God is at work in all Christians, not just in the clergy, who dominate traditional churches.
- All believers are more than volunteers; the Spirit moves them to minister to others.
- The most basic leadership job in a church is to build up the fellowship of the Holy Spirit, not just to edify believers.
- There is no one master plan for growth in the Spirit; the Spirit from Christ adapts to our individual personalities and experiences.

This book doesn't offer a master plan, but it features the six common-sense practices mentioned earlier. By doing them believers can welcome the Spirit to grow his gifts in them:

1. *Go* to God in worship and prayer.
2. *Receive* God's word for you.
3. *Own* your self-denial.
4. Give *witness* to your experiences.
5. *Trust* God in a new venture.

6. *Humble* yourself before God.

These steps work best when shared with other believers. Hence I am emphasizing small-group partnerships, in which those in each regularly share their experiences, preferably once a week for several weeks. Enough small groups over time will add up to a whole congregation regularly sharing such experiences of *growth* in the Spirit together. This is what Paul envisioned for the congregations he formed and led. Joy and thankfulness will be more evident in congregations that celebrate such GROWTH.

A renewed emphasis on the work of the Spirit in lives today will mean a change in the leadership model common among old-line churches. The old shepherd model of ministry as feeding and leading Christians is outmoded. Better is a development model, such as the planter, gardener, and builder Paul saw himself to be.

I have framed the following chapters as discussions among participants in a partnership that comes together regularly to seek better understanding of how the Spirit works.

Here is how I have organized the book:

Park 1: Naming the Issues

Part 2: Recognizing How the Spirit Works Today

Part 3: Growing in the Spirit

Part 4: Leading Spiritual Growth in a Congregation

Discussion Questions

1. When you think of something as being "spiritual," what meaning does that have for you? How have you separated "spiritual" from "unspiritual"?
2. Jesus explained that he came to give "abundant" life. What are your thoughts about the abundant life in Christ?
3. Have you heard of the "gifts of the Spirit" before? Which of these gifts would you like to receive?
4. 4. Are there any "thriving" Protestant churches in your neighborhood? What is distinctive about them?
5. 5. Are you aware of any "withering" churches? Are you aware of any efforts to halt decline and turn them around?

Discussion 2

The Spirit and the Easy Yoke

Offering special events to help believers become better disciples of Jesus is a hard sell in the congregations I know. It's one of those things in the Christian life that you know you should do someday, but for the most part, it seems like another burden for already busy and weary lives.

But what if the burden were light? What if following Jesus could be made easy? Jesus himself said that those who come to him will find a light burden and an easy yoke. Come to him to rest.[14]

This is the same Jesus who told his disciples, "If anyone would come after me, he must deny himself and take up his cross daily." He followed up that challenge with this riddle: "For whoever wants to save his life will lose it, but whoever loses his life for me will save it."[15]

He expected his disciples to give up life as they knew it. During their remaining time with Jesus, they mostly saw a heavy burden and hard yoke they fundamentally didn't understand. And so they were crushed when the Messiah died and left them on their own.

It wasn't until fifty days after Jesus's resurrection that his disciples recalled words Jesus had spoken during his meal with them before his death. He wouldn't leave them alone on their own. He promised to send the Spirit to come alongside them and teach and guide them into all truth Jesus represented. At Pentecost this Spirit moved mightily among them. Then they began to understand the puzzle. They gladly left their old life behind for the joy of living in God's grace.

The key to Jesus's analogy is the yoke. A yoke is used to spread the burden over at least two animals pulling the load. Instead of being on our own to live out the heavy and costly

David S. Luecke

burden of true discipleship, God freely gives us someone who can help us carry the load. This is Jesus's Spirit, the Holy Spirit. He is named the *paraklete*—someone who comes alongside, like parallel. The Spirit comes alongside the believer to share the yoke. He is continually at work, changing our hearts so we increasingly find joy in living the way of Jesus Christ.

In scripture the yoke usually stands for the burden of expectations we face, often summarized as the law, represented by the Pharisees and their 613 rules for successfully pleasing God. For the former Pharisee, Paul, the law of the Spirit now replaced those laws. They release me from the oppression of obligations I can't meet—the heavy yoke.[16] Paul taught us that the Lord Jesus is the Spirit, and where the Spirit is, there is freedom.[17] There also is joy, peace, and hope—the light yoke. Furthermore, the gifts of the Spirit enable followers, who are saved by grace, to live by grace as well.

We believers find ourselves living out two contrasting stories. One is our human instinct to rely on ourselves to become better disciples—the hard way. The other is to look for the Holy Spirit's help to follow the easy way. The hard way on our own drains our energy because the burden is heavy. The other way is easy because the Spirit changes and empowers us for the adventures of our personal journey into the abundant life Jesus came to give. Paul described that life as experiencing ever-greater love, peace, and joy; and reflecting more and more of the glory of God.[18] The difference can be difficult to recognize until the Spirit helps us to see with eyes of the heart he is changing.[19]

How the Spirit makes the yoke easier can be hard to understand because the process seems counterintuitive. Others can help explain it more fully. Let me share descriptions by John Ortberg, John Eldridge, Dallas Willard, John Koenig, Gordon Fee, and the apostle Paul. I have been in discussions with them through their books.

16

John Ortberg

Pastor and clinical psychologist John Ortberg describes this contrast as between living the "me" others want me to be and living the "me" I want to be. He purposefully doesn't aim for the "me" God wants me to be because our expectations of what God wants are the issue. He isn't focused on the egotistical "me" but the unique "me" God created and the "me" made new in Christ by the Spirit. God's plan isn't just for us to be *saved* by grace—it is for us to *live* by grace. For many of us Christians, the meaning of God's grace *in this life* can be confusing.

Ortberg describes the satisfactions that come from living in the flow of the Spirit. Jesus himself gave that image: "Let anyone who is thirsty come to me and drink. Whoever believes in me streams of living water will flow from within them. By this Jesus meant the Spirit, whom his followers were later to receive."[20] "Flowing in the Spirit" is Ortberg's phrase for the stream that nourishes and gives power so we can become the person God designed. "You become 'you-ier.' When I am in the flow of the Spirit, sin looks bad and God looks good. When I experience gratitude, contentment, and satisfaction deep in my soul, there is a good chance it is the Spirit flowing within. I can't make myself loving or joyful. When I am in the flow of the Spirit I am moved toward greater love and more joy. And the blessing does not stop with me. The Spirit never just flows in us; he always flows through us so that others might flourish as well."

Further, Ortberg asks, how do you keep yourself aware and submitted to God's Spirit so that rivers of living water flow through your belly, through the core of your being? Just don't quench the Spirit, Paul answered. "The Spirit is already at work in you. Jesus said that if you are a follower of his, the Spirit is there. He is bigger than you; he is stronger than you; he is more patient with your failures, gaps, inadequacies, and pretending than you are. He is committed to helping you 24–7. Your only job is not getting in his way."[21]

A major goal for this present book is to help believers grow in the Spirit. I intend that process to be what John Ortberg describes in his distinctive way. God never grows two people the same way. God is a hand crafter, not a mass producer. The problem many people face is that they listen to someone they think of as the expert—maybe the pastor of their church—talk about what he does and think that is what they are supposed to do. When it doesn't work for them—because they are a different person—they feel guilty and inadequate; they often give up.

Hear John Ortberg when he assures you that the main measure of your devotion to God isn't your devotional life. It is simply your life. A spiritual discipline is simply an activity you engage in to be made more fully alive by the Spirit of life.

John Eldridge

Author of *The Sacred Romance,* John Eldridge is a Christian counselor and speaker who invites us to live out the "sacred romance," because the Christian life is a love affair of the heart. Many of us Christians hear a small, passionate voice that tells us we haven't been diligent enough in practicing our religion. Rather, listen to the voice that wants to say there is something missing in your routine Christian life. Life in our modern world has taught all of us to ignore and distrust the deepest yearning of our hearts and to live only in the external world where efficiency and performance are everything. But the life of the heart is a place of great mystery. God made you for something more. The Christian life is meant to be a love affair, an adventure.

The fundamental story, according to Eldridge, is the wildness of God's loving heart shown in the drama he has been weaving since before the beginning of time. His heart was betrayed when sin entered the world. When we turned our backs on him, he promised to come for us. He sent personal messengers; he used beauty and affliction to recapture our hearts. After all else failed, he conceived the most daring of plans—sending his Son to offer a way to restoration. Now God's heart is on trial, as he woos each of us back. He actually wants to give us, his beloved, our freedom, which we are free to reject.

In return, what does God want from us? Eldridge observes that often we're told that what God wants is obedience, sacrifice, adherence to the right doctrines, or proper morality. True, but what he is really after is *us*—our laughter, tears, dreams, fears, or heart of hearts. How few of us truly believe this. We've never been wanted for our hearts, our truest selves, not really, not for long. The thought that God wants our hearts seems too good to be true. It's like a fairy tale. But this fairy tale is real and true.[22]

What is the result of the sacred romance as it plays out in each life? We find that our way of living starts to change. We lift our sights beyond ourselves to focus on others. Here is how Jesus said it (in the Message translation): "When a person lives merely to preserve his life, he eventually loses it altogether. Rather, give your life away and discover life as it was always meant to be. Self–preservation is no help at all. Self-sacrifice is the way, my way, to finding yourself, your true self."[23] Living the greater story is a light burden because he who seeks us sends his Spirit to empower us for fulfilled living. The Spirit makes Christ's yoke easy.

Dallas Willard

Many of my discussions in recent years have been with Dallas Willard through his books. I admire him highly as an accomplished professional philosopher who deeply understands the Christian life and has a flare for challenging misleading popular assumptions about life in Christ.

He explains how formation by the Spirit involves much more than human effort and actions under our control. Well-informed human effort certainly is indispensable, for spiritual formation isn't a passive process. But the Christlikeness of the inner being isn't a human attainment. It is, finally, a gift of grace.[24]

Willard explains why we aren't told in any systematic way how to make progress in God's kingdom. This is because the process is to be a walk with a person. But it is also because what is needed is very much an individual matter, a response to the particular need of individual disciples. That is why we don't find precise details in the Bible. The specifics of this process will be modeled and picked up by the devoted individual from the group, from redemptive history and from the good sense of humankind. And that is exactly what we see when we look at the history of Jesus's people.[25]

John Koenig

New Testament scholar John Koenig finds two striking features in his study of *God's Gifts for God's People*. The first is that the individual recipient has to be interested enough in God's gifts to want them and to want them from God. There is a consciousness in us, however minimal, of a God close at hand who is constantly trying to break through to us with his gifts.

The second common feature in the New Testament accounts is that gifts are always given in the presence of at least one other person, usually more. It is this insight that lays the foundation for this present book's encouragement to find partners to name and share experiences of the Spirit.[26]

Gordon Fee

The undisputed expert today on Paul and the Spirit, Gordon Fee presents an almost one-thousand-page study of *God's Empowering Presence*. I have spent recent years studying his detailed analysis and summary of the 143 passages on the Spirit's work in Paul's letters.

Fee's study is a book on Paul's theology as he and his churches experienced it. The Spirit stood much closer to the center of things for him—and for them—than seems to be true for us. The Spirit, as an experienced and living reality, was the absolutely crucial matter for Christian life, from beginning to end. "Despite the affirmations in our creeds and hymns and the lip service paid to the Spirit in our occasional conversations, the Spirit is largely marginalized in our actual life together as a community of faith." He approves of the observation by now-famous N. T. Wright that Paul's doctrine of the Spirit is far more central and characteristic than his doctrine of justification by faith.[27]

Discussions with the Apostle Paul

Over the years my admiration for the apostle Paul has grown, especially for his approach to leadership, the subject of my academic specialty as taught to MBAs and pastors. But leadership and administration can be boring to people who don't see a need to move beyond traditional ways of doing things.

What's called for is the prior step of helping them see fresh energy that needs active leadership, leadership that in turn needs to see beyond tradition to clarify where special church energy comes from. I discovered in the process that the Spirit's special energy is much more exciting to talk about than how to manage just human effort.

We don't know much about the twelve years of Paul's life after his dramatic conversion and the beginning of his ministry with Barnabas. I think he roamed in and around Tarsus, preaching and trying to explain God's wonderful action in turning around his life. God inspired his special formulations of the divine gift of grace to enter the next life but especially his gifts for living an exciting life now.

Along the way in those years, God brought about more changes in Paul's life that he recorded in his letters. Through the work of the Spirit, he found in himself the following:

- Movement beyond childhood knowledge to greater willingness to live with Jesus as Lord of his life
- Less inclination to gratify desires of his old sinful nature
- Less feelings of pervasive fears that inhibit joyful living
- Experiences of a spiritual act of worship in decisions to sacrifice what seemed important to live a life more pleasing to God
- Experiences of a special sense of unity with other believers

- Increased feelings of love, joy, peace, patience, and gentleness
- The frustration of speaking only words of human wisdom and the privilege to express spiritual truths in spiritual words[28]

Discussions with Myself

My own life experiences predisposed me to appreciate Paul's emphasis on how the power to change comes from outside oneself, explainable for Christians in the work of the Spirit. Academic success came early. My lifelong signature sin would be pride in what I could accomplish. Several professional incidents that looked like failure taught me to humble myself before God and appreciate Jesus's challenge to deny myself.

A developer by temperament, I have learned to trust God's providence. Many of my "kingdom adventures" didn't work out as I had intended. But the important ones did, such as planting a church that somebody else could build up better than I. I am trusting God that something good will come out of my recent writing efforts. For me these are a spiritual discipline.

My 2014 book *Encounters with the Holy Spirit: Name and Share Them—Seek More* laid out a more theoretical understanding of the Spirit's work today. It includes perspectives from the sociological and psychological sciences, which have been a special interest of mine since receiving the PhD in organizational behavior at Washington University in St. Louis. This present book concentrates on more practical applications.

How the Spirit changes lives is something I have observed in myself personally over many years. I grew from an aggressive, fast-track vice chancellor at a major university to a much-mellowed pastor who learned to wait on opportunities the Spirit granted in God's timing. I have experienced the fruit of the Spirit growing in my life and along the way have experienced much more love, joy, peace, and patience.

The six practices for growth in the Spirit work, at least for me.

Part 2: Recognizing How the Spirit Works Today

Discussion 3

Naming Encounters with the Spirit

What does the Holy Spirit look like? We can envision God as a Father and Jesus as a Son. What about a Holy *Ghost*, the name used before modern translations? Casper the Ghost was popular when I was a kid. What's a kid supposed to think about this ghost person of the Trinity? What's an adult supposed to think? At least Casper was friendly.

Gordon Fee observes, "We confess *tri*-nitarian belief in God the Father, the Son and the Holy Spirit, but we practice *bi*-nitarian ministry, looking mainly to the Father and Son. Most see the Spirit as a gray blur, a ghostly presence hovering in the background."

At the Son's baptism in the River Jordon, the Father's voice said of Jesus, "This is my own dear Son, with whom I am pleased."[29] As he came up out of the water, Jesus saw the Spirit of God coming down like a dove and lighting on him. Envision the Spirit as that dove sitting on his shoulder. Now he is doing that on *your* shoulder, whispering in *your* ear.

So far I have been addressing you, the reader. Stay with me as I switch to a discussion I'm having with an imaginary small group of believers. They have accepted my invitation to come together to learn about growth in the Spirit. I am encouraging them to become partners in doing the practices for growth in the Spirit. Explained in Discussion 8, these practices are identified in the acronym GROWTH. A reality of the faith life is that we really do grow in the Spirit better when we share experiences with others.

Some of the participants are Rick, Amy, John, Amber, Bill, Gail, Ed, Sarah, and Jim. I am Dave.

Jesus Explained the Spirit's Work

Dave: Jesus gave the job description for the Spirit shortly before his death and resurrection. As the evangelist John related, "I will ask the Father and he will give you another Counselor to be with you for ever—the Spirit of truth. You know him because he lives with you and will be in you. I will not leave you as orphans. This Counselor, the Spirit, will teach you all things and remind you of everything I have said to you."[30] Also, "Unless I go away, the Counselor will not come to you. When I go, I will send him to you. He will bring glory to me by taking from what is mine and making it known to you."[31]

The original word is *parakletos*, usually seen as the comforting counselor. I will focus more on the counselor who advocates the ways and thoughts of the Father and Son, who have been sending him throughout the centuries since Jesus's ascension back to the right hand of the Father.

The word *parakletos* also shows up in the first letter of John to describe Jesus Christ's job. We have an advocate who speaks to the Father in our defense—Jesus Christ, who is the atoning sacrifice for our sins. Pairing the advocacies makes a neat symmetry. Christ is now in heaven, advocating our cause before the Father. The Spirit now is among us on earth, advocating the Father and Son's cause in our lives.

John: The Spirit as counselor I know. Those passages from the Gospel of John are read at Pentecost in my church. But I will have to admit we don't hear much about the Spirit the rest of the year.

Dave: It is easy to think of the counselor as someone you go to when you are having troubles. And indeed making the comfort of the gospel personal is a big part of the Spirit's work. But the *paraklete* as an advocate opens up more possibilities.

John: I like the image of Jesus as our advocate before the Father.

Dave: Right now that is what he is doing. He sits at the right hand of the Father saying, "I died for that one. She or he belongs to me." In turn, both the Father and the Son send the Spirit to be their advocate for the more abundant life Jesus came to offer. They always have more blessings in store for us than we can imagine.

Jesus himself explained to Nicodemus what the Spirit accomplishes: "No one can enter the kingdom of God unless he is born of water and the Spirit. Flesh gives birth to flesh, the Holy Spirit gives birth to human spirit." The Spirit influences human spirits. We become different when the Spirit works on and in us.

Paul Explained the Spirit's Work

One short verse in Paul's first letter to the Corinthians can open up a whole new perspective for traditional Christians. "But eagerly desire the greater gifts. And now I will show you the most excellent way."

This description comes at the end of chapter 12, which starts with Paul's statement of intent to explain "spiritual gifts." The "lesser" gifts are "manifestations of the Spirit given for the common good" of a congregation. The "greater" gifts are faith, hope, and especially love, which Paul described in chapter 13 with great eloquence in one of the all-time favorite passages in scripture.

New appreciation for love, faith, and hope opens up when they are associated with Paul's description of fruit of the Spirit, such as love, joy, peace, patience, kindness, goodness, faithfulness, gentleness, and self-control.[32] What do these words describe? Usually they are considered virtues associated with life in Christ. I believe Paul described feelings or inner dispositions of hearts the Spirit challenged.

New appreciation for the lesser gifts can come by seeing them as motivations of members to contribute their special abilities to the work and life of believers gathered as a church. He gives these examples: "We have different gifts, according to the grace given us. If a man's gift is proclaiming, let him us it in proportion to this faith. If it is serving, let him serve; if it is teaching, let him teach; If it is encouraging, let him encourage; if it is contributing to the needs of others, let him give generously; if it is leadership, let him govern diligently; if it is showing mercy, let him do it cheerfully."[33]

Diane: What you are saying makes sense. Why is this a whole new perspective?

Dave: Because over the centuries the heavily institutionalized Christian church narrowed down the Spirit's influence to what they could control. Over time spiritual motivation was attributed to clergy with little expected of others beyond their participation in spiritual rituals conducted by the clergy.

The Reformers recovered a greater role for all believers, even though they continued the emphasis on clergy. I think they also didn't know what to do with the special gifts of speaking in tongues and working miracles. John Calvin specifically taught that supernatural miracles ceased after the New Testament church.

John: I was in a church once when a fellow burst out with strange sounds that made no sense. It almost freaked me out.

Dave: I understand speaking in tongues to be a prayer language by which the Spirit intercedes for us with groans that words cannot express. But I haven't seen persuasive evidence that the speaker is actually talking in an intelligible language he or she didn't know previously.

Amy: Do you think miracles really happen today?

Dave: In defense of the Reformers, they lived in a time of lots of superstitions in a world of strange beings out there trying to influence them. Yes, I have become convinced that miracles do occasionally happen today. I present some evidence in my book *Your Encounters with the Holy Spirit*.[34]

Why the Reformers continued to overlook the fruit of the Spirit has a different explanation. They were part of the long Western intellectual heritage of looking down on emotions, which aren't a reliable guide for decision-making. It is better to rely on careful reasoning about biblical truths. Hence the appeal to heads. They didn't have the modern understanding of how inner dispositions guide so much of our behavior. We have much greater appreciation for "hearts" and motivations than they did.

Sarah: Are you saying, for instance, that the meaning of "love" was much simpler for them?

Dave: Again, a long tradition saw love as simply attraction for someone or something and could be rationally explained. We know so much more is involved. We also know it does little good to command someone to love his or her neighbor. The inner disposition has to be there. Hearts have to change. Listen to Jesus and Paul when they explained that changing hearts is the specialty of the Spirit.

27

There is yet another reason the Spirit's work in the present isn't well understood. The Reformers focused on Jesus Christ and on how Paul described what life "in Christ" is like. But Paul didn't make a clear distinction between what Christ did for us in his life, death, and resurrection and what the Spirit does for us now.

Seeing the Spirit as the spirit of Christ, Paul used the two interchangeably as opposite sides of the same coin. Having the Spirit in us and having Christ in us are one and the same thing. See the merger at work in these pairings:

Eph. 2:18

1st Cor. 2:11

1st John 2:27

> We are sealed in Christ; we are sealed in the Holy Spirit.
>
> We are consecrated in Christ; we are consecrated in the Holy Spirit.
>
> We are righteous in Christ; we are righteous in the Holy Spirit.
>
> We have life through Christ; we have life through the Spirit.
>
> We have hope grounded in Christ; we have hope grounded in the power of the Spirit.
>
> Christ is the alternative to the Law; the Spirit is the alternative to the Law.

Gal. 5:22-23 no law

Fruit

> We are to stand fast in the Lord; we are to stand fast in the one Spirit.
>
> We are to rejoice in the Lord; we have joy in the Holy Spirit.
>
> We are told to live in Christ; we are told to walk in the Spirit.

Paul speaks the truth in the Christ; Paul speaks the truth in the Spirit.

We are called into the fellowship of Christ; we are blessed with the fellowship of the Holy Spirit. (citations are in endnote[35])

Rick: I have always been confused about where the Spirit fits in. I understand being grounded in Christ. Being grounded in the Spirit is new to me.

Dave: I, too, was confused until I read Lewis Smede's book *Union with Christ*. He put together the pairings I just listed. The phrase "in Christ" was a favorite of Paul as he explained the basics of life with God after Jesus's life, death, and resurrection. According to my Greek concordance, Paul used that phrase eighty-one times in his writing.[36] But in Gordon Fee's analysis, Paul referred to the Holy Spirit more often—143 times.[37] The goal then and now is to live "in Christ." The power to do that is from the Holy Spirit.

Smedes concludes, "The Spirit is Christ in action. The Spirit is Christ as he is experienced in and by the church. The Spirit is Christ in the present time."[38]

More or Less of the Spirit

I want to share one more observation for how the Spirit influences believers today that can help us spot him at work in us or others. We find it in Luke's Gospel and his Book of Acts. He used the phrase that someone was "full of the Holy Spirit" and then identified how this was made evident.

Thus, full of the Holy Spirit:

- Elizabeth rejoiced (Luke 1:4).
- Zechariah prophesized (Luke 1:67).
- Peter had unusual courage (Luke 4:8).
- The seven table helpers had unusual wisdom (Luke 4:13).

29

- Stephen had special trust for the next life (Luke 7:55).
- Barnabas had trust in the Antioch church (Acts 11:24).
- Disciples were filled with joy and the Holy Spirit (Luke 13:52).

The Holy Spirit is always within all believers. But under some circumstances, he motivates someone to unusual levels of God-pleasing behavior. You might remember times in your faith life when you found yourself overflowing with trust, joy, or confidence. I hope you will share such experiences a little later.

When looking for the Holy Spirit, recognize that the Spirit's gifts of changed feelings and motivations are at the core of what he gives Christ's followers today.

Naming the Spirit's Movement in and around You

Dave: Here is a definition I have developed for how to recognize the Spirit at work in you or others. It is rather stiff, but I want to get it right.

Recognize the Holy Spirit at work in situations where

(a) you experience, observe, or remember God's love working and Christ's grace healing; and where

(b) you or others react with better understanding of God's ways and/or with special feelings like peace, joy, awe, unity, or fresh energy to serve.

Part a is the situations where the Spirit is active. Part b is the response from you or someone else. In future discussions we will talk about how to grow in the Spirit's influence. A quick answer is to put yourself where the Spirit can work on you. The spiritual practices for GROWTH in the Spirit are designed for that purpose.

Jesus came so we could have a joyful, abundant life. He

30

usually described this as living in the kingdom of God—the reign of God in our hearts. This kingdom starts as a seed and grows to take over more and more of the believer's life. Such growth is the work of the Spirit. We can expect the Spirit to enrich our lives with the richness of God's grace, "which he lavishes on us with all wisdom and understanding."[39]

This kingdom is all about God's love working and Christ's grace healing—a simplified way of summarizing the gospel. When you see God's love and healing having an effect on yourself or others, you have evidence of the Spirit's action. He works on heads to bring about greater understanding of God's desired impact on people. The Spirit also works on hearts to arouse special feelings in response to God's actions. The Spirit influences with heads and hearts combined to arouse special energy and desire in us to extend the kingdom by serving others in the name of Christ.

The feelings include not only what Paul described as fruit of the Spirit but also unusual awe at his majesty or a sense of unusual unity with others of the faith. Such unity is a product of the Spirit's distinctive characteristic of fellowship builder.

Feelings ran strong among God's people in the Bible. The psalmists specialized in expressing in words their feelings about God and their life situations. King David did this unusually well. He put memorable words about his experience of the depth of despair in Psalm 130: "Out of the depths I cry to you, O Lord." He described the sorrows of repentance in Psalm 51: "Have mercy on me, O God, blot out my transgressions." By far the Twenty-third Psalm is the most popular one: "The Lord is my shepherd." Note these feelings phrases: "I shall not want," "I will feel no evil," "You bring me to green pastures and quiet waters," "You restore my soul and comfort me with your rod and staff," "You make my cup overflow," "Goodness and love will follow me," and "I will dwell in the house of the Lord forever."

Amber: That psalm brings to mind the feelings I saw and experienced at my grandmother's funeral. My family's emotions were heavy.

Dave: It is no coincidence that Psalm 23 is requested at all funerals.

It is in singing hymns that you can most easily observe the Spirit working on your feelings. Let's share later the ones that work best on you. Some that arouse strong feelings in me are "I know that my Redeemer lives" and "This is Holy Ground."

I have to tell you about my experience several years ago when I led a group on a tour of Israel. When we got to the Sea of Galilee, a boat took us out a ways on the sea where we could see so many of the places Jesus had taught and ministered. The operator then loudly played a recording of "How Great Thou Art," and we all sang—with more and more gusto. Among people I know in that setting, my emotions overflowed. The experience blew me away, and I am not a very emotional person. We were filled with the Spirit and awe, joy, and unity.

What made that experience so memorable was the coming together of at least four circumstances that triggered the emotion. One was seeing the actual ground where Jesus walked and taught. Another was the unusual feel of the water at that very special place. Add strong memories of singing that favorite hymn. Yet another was doing this in the company of fellow church people, whose faith I knew. Any one of those forces would have triggered a special emotion. Put them together, and the Spirit moved mightily.

Trigger Situations

By trigger I mean a special event or circumstance in which the strong movement of the Spirit was experienced. I told you of Luke's phrase that in a specific situation a biblical person was full of the Holy Spirit and special power. Elizabeth was Spirit filled with joy when Mary shared her good news. The trigger for Zechariah's Spirit-filled prophecy about the Messiah was being asked for the name of Elizabeth's baby and giving the name John. The seven table helpers were filled with the Spirit and wisdom. Appearing before the hostile Sanhedrin was the occasion when Peter, full of the Holy Spirit, spoke boldly. When Barnabas encouraged the church in Antioch, they recognized in him a special Spirit-filled trust of God's work in this new church.

Can you envision a situation when you were called on to do or say something in the name of Christ and felt special empowerment?

What are some trigger events for Christians today? Think about your feelings during worship on Easter morning. Or perhaps when receiving the body and blood of Christ at the celebration of the Lord's Supper at church. Or times in personal prayer when you experience God's peace and presence. From research I did among ordinary churchgoers, I know that half reported that their times in personal prayer were the most satisfying experience in their lives. Or maybe it was a time when you thought about God's love as you or someone else noticed and helped a person in special need. Recognize these as triggers that happen in routine life in Christ.

Gail: I remember the sense of satisfaction I got when a young mom ahead of me in the checkout lane didn't have enough money to pay for the basic things in her cart. I stepped forward to pay for all of it. It just seemed like a basic act of Christian love. I felt good, and it made me thankful for all that I have.

Dave: Some other triggering circumstances might be whispers of the Spirit, a time of grief or loss, an experience of conversion or awakening, and rarely a near-death experience.

By a whisper of the Spirit, I mean a time when a thought popped into your head that you should go visit a specific person, and it turned out this was the right time and right place specifically for you to be there. Those triggers were probably whispers of the Spirit. Many I talk to can recall such whispers. They are relieved to talk about those moments as messages from God.

Times of special loss can trigger an encounter with the Spirit. Earlier Amber mentioned the strong emotions at her grandmother's funeral. The death of someone close to you can be a good time to review in your mind your beliefs about God, his creation of humans, the gospel facts, and their meaning for human life here and in eternity. A serious illness can trigger that same kind of review of beliefs and bring a new level of trust and peace. I have seen how losing a job can bring worry about security and stimulate a new appreciation for God's providence and faithfulness.

Of course the Spirit is at work in a conversion to the Christian faith or a profound awakening in that faith. For some this is gradual. For others it can be a memorable event, perhaps even at a specific time and place. For infant-baptized Christians, this is really an awakening to faith into which they were baptized. Conversion and awakening can look similar. Either way such a story is worth sharing with others. Mainline churches haven't learned how to do that. Sharing such stories can increase the effectiveness of our witness and be an encouragement to others in the faith.

In the previous book, I described the long process I went through to gain confidence that God really can intervene in natural processes with an event for which there is no natural explanation. Call such an event a "miracle." For those willing to see such evidence of God's power today, such an event can be a tremendous boost to their faith. Healings are seen as the special providence of the Holy Spirit. Most mainline Christians are primed not to recognize such supernatural interventions. Indeed, they are rare. But experiencing or witnessing one can give increased confidence that God is near now, not just in Bible times.

Bill: Thanks for this explanation. But I am skeptical about the Spirit's involvement in such experiences. They could be explained by routine psychology.

Dave: As well you should be skeptical. Too many Christians are gullible for whatever extreme view someone claims. Coincidence can explain away anything unusual happening. But as more evidence accumulates from otherwise-reasonable people, you do have to eventually conclude that something out of the ordinary is happening. If you're going to be a Christian, you might as well recognize the biblical explanation: the Spirit is at work among us.

One last category of a trigger to an encounter with the Spirit is near-death experiences and their glimpses of the afterlife. Such stories have happened for centuries, but in recent decades they are making their way into popular literature. Unfortunately, a few are faked. But many are plausible in the details given. One I have the most confidence in is *Proof of Heaven: A Neurosurgeon's Journey in the Afterlife* (2012) by Dr. Eben Alexander. As a neurologist, he had specialized knowledge of how to interpret the medical records. He was really dead, and he is fully recovered.

One near-death experience is related by James Loder, who was then a junior faculty member at Princeton Seminary. He was pinned beneath his automobile in an accident, and his wife rescued him. Then he was "never more conscious of the life that poured through me, nor more aware that this life was not my own." He spent the rest of his academic career trying to understand and explain what happened. Here are two of his conclusions: no one can know or comprehend the central meaning of a convicting experience from a standpoint outside of it. It is intensely personal. Also, the validation of a word from God is uniformly established by God's initiative, not by generally recognized human procedures. He thinks theological

[handwritten margin right, top] after 19, Nothing left.

[handwritten margin right] Dad (Carl Byrd) experienced a moment of "loss of everything he ever did or was. everything"

[handwritten margin right, lower] Dad 4/23/19

[handwritten margin bottom left] I know! My boy was at the cross! the cross! 7/4/1994

repression is a good word for what happens in a church culture that isn't open to God's supernatural interventions.[40]

I am encouraged that near-death experiences are receiving increased attention in popular culture. These accounts are now even receiving serious research attention.[41]

Can you prove beyond a doubt that such encounters are experiences of the Spirit? No. Someone who doesn't believe God exists or that he is active in life today won't be persuaded by evidence for something he or she cannot or won't recognize. Nor will research ever be done to the highest standard of scientific inquiry because the variable of God's input cannot be measured consistently. But I am delighted that people in the scientific community accept the plausibility of God's interventions enough to put effort into researching the subject. I am encouraged by that   *Romans 11:33 Unsearchable*

The biblical John in his first letter warned, "Do not believe every spirit, but test the spirits to see whether they are from God." Here is the test: "Every Spirit that acknowledges that Jesus Christ has come in the flesh is from God."[42] Those that don't aren't from God. Here are some signs of the Spirit at work: a new nature apparent through lives that show a difference, a reflection of love of God that doesn't come from self-interest, a genuine humility, a hunger for God, and a Christlike Spirit. Centuries ago, Jonathan Edwards identified these signs at a time when emotions ran high in the first Great Awakening in America.

We will talk more about fruit of the Spirit in Discussion 4 and special motivation in Discussion 5.

Discussion Questions

1. Before today, how have you envisioned the Spirit and what he does?
2. 2. Have you ever experienced the Holy Spirit as God's comforter?

3. Have you ever known a Christian who seemed especially "spiritual" in terms of an extra measure of wisdom, courage, or generosity?
4. Is the careful definition of an encounter with the Holy Spirit offered earlier in this chapter helpful to you?
5. What might be special occasions or places that trigger in you strong feelings about your faith and your God?

7-3-19

Discussion 4

Living the Present Salvation of the Spirit's Fruit

When teaching the fruit of the Spirit, I ask, "Who right now wouldn't want to have more love, joy, peace, patience, kindness, goodness, faithfulness, gentleness, and self-control?" The answer, of course, is that all would like such feelings all the time. Parents of young children usually list patience as their top priority.

Is it just possible that these feeling outcomes are the point of the gospel for followers of Jesus while they are still in this life? If so, facilitating such working of Christ's Spirit would be central to the lives of those gathered as the church of Christ. Of course, Jesus's death and resurrection ensure eternal life after we leave this physical one. That is the total gospel. Meanwhile, according to Paul, we have the benefit of these first fruits of the Spirit here and now.[43]

Living the fruit of the Spirit gives added meaning to Jesus's own explanation of his purpose. "I am come that they have life, and have it to the full."[44] How much better can life get than to live full of love, joy, peace, kindness, gentleness, and similar descriptions of what the Spirit wants to bring into the lives of Christ followers? Actually the original word *full* means "full to overflowing."

Join me as I ask the participants in the small group, "What would the abundant life look like for you?"

Bill: Well, having more money would sure help. But I suspect that I am not supposed to say that here.

Dave: True, Jesus talked a lot about money and how the love of it can really mess up someone's life. But here is another reason. Studies of happiness have become a major topic of research for psychologists in recent years. One consistent finding is that, above a minimal survival level, more money and stuff don't bring lasting happiness. We adjust quickly and just want more.

Sarah: I would like to overflow with love, especially being loved by others. But relationships get complicated, and I often feel disappointed.

Dave: It is this area of relationships that opens up new possibilities. Another consistent finding is that people in faith communities generally score higher on happiness scales. For Christians that means relationships with other believers, usually in a congregation, but especially a relationship with Jesus Christ, who cares deeply about those who follow him. This relationship is brought closer by the Spirit in our prayers that he prompts.

What we talk about as happiness the Bible describes as being blessed. Jesus's description of those who are blessed is in Matthew 5. Take a moment to read the beatitudes in verses 3–9.

Consider the description of those who are called happy: "the poor in spirit, ... those who mourn, ... the meek, ... those who hunger and thirst after righteousness, ... the merciful, ... the pure in heart, ... the peacemakers, ... those who are persecuted because of their righteousness."

What do you see as the common denominator?

Amy: That's a hard one. I suppose they aren't the ones you would usually associate with being happy—like those who mourn, the meek, the persecuted, and maybe even the merciful. You don't usually think of weakness bringing happiness.

Dave: Yes, but God's way is different. Two observations. One is that almost all these are people in a relationship with others, and it is their special posture that makes them blessed. The other is that the first posture shapes all the others: blessed are the poor in spirit. In their human spirit, they know their faults and inadequacies. In short, they are humble.

Bob: Are you implying that the proud are usually unhappy?

Dave: Right on. They come at life with an attitude shaped around what they deserve, an attitude certainly bolstered by our consumer, rights-oriented society. One of the consistent messages of the Bible is that God resists the proud but has mercy on the humble. A basic finding in psychology is that expectations determine much of satisfaction in work and life. Self-centered, inflated expectations lead to chronic unhappiness.

Rick: We started this discussion with your question of what would be the abundant life Jesus promised his followers. Are you saying the abundant life is available only to followers of Jesus?

Dave: When we mean the abundant life overflowing with love, joy, peace, and the other positive feelings, the answer is yes. Let me tell you why. Everyone has some of those feeling some of the time. But Paul taught us to regard such feelings as fruit of the Spirit. The Spirit has a primary job before he can work these positive outcomes. He has to change hearts. Some call this "conversion." Better to call it repentance—humbling ourselves before God and rejecting all our sinful self-centeredness that messes up so many of our relationships. Through this humbling of ourselves, we renew our right standing with him.

Some say this happens once in a lifetime. It is a strength of infant-baptizing churches to see this as even a daily event—putting down our old nature and letting the new nature come forth, the new spiritual nature of those who walk with Christ's Spirit. This is what Paul meant when he wrote to Titus, "[God] saved us through the washing of rebirth and renewal by the Holy Spirit, whom he poured out on us generously through Jesus Christ our Savior."[45]

Paul had daily life in mind when he wished for the Christians in Rome that "the God of hope [would] fill you with all joy and peace as you trust in him, so that you may overflow with hope by the power of the Spirit."[46] Jesus went about proclaiming that the kingdom of God is at hand, and he meant God's rule in the hearts of his people. Certainly this means the kingdom of heaven for eternity, but this rule begins in this present life for followers of Christ. Paul explains again to the Romans that the kingdom of God isn't a matter of rules, like what you eat or drink, "but of righteousness, peace and joy in the Holy Spirit."[47]

Now, here's a new question about salvation. What does the word *saved* mean?

Amber: To me it means we will be saved from hell to spend eternity with God in heaven. I think of my favorite passage: "God so loved the world that he gave his only begotten son that whosoever believes in him should not perish but have eternal life."[48]

Dave: Absolutely. This is God's most basic promise for those who accept Jesus as their Savior. Would it surprise you, though, to learn that "salvation" in the New Testament has several meanings? Jesus used the same original word *sōzō* when he told the bleeding woman, "Your faith has healed you," and Luke explained that she was healed from that moment. To be saved can mean to be healed. That same word was used again when the disciples in a boat with Jesus feared for their lives and woke him up with the plea,

"Lord, save us! We're going to drown!" Jesus then calmed the storm. To be saved is to be rescued from present danger.

John: These other meanings are new for me.

Dave: Let me show you where this insight can go.

Reformers Martin Luther and John Calvin missed this insight about the abundant life as present salvation. They were preoccupied with questions of eternal salvation in a medieval world where hell, purgatory, and heaven were pressing realities that shaped how people lived—attaining the rewards of one and avoiding the tortures of the other. The defining issue was *how* such eternal salvation happens.

Amber: Where I will be for eternity is important to me. That is why I like John 3:16. Those who believe in Christ will not perish but have eternal life.

Dave: You have been a lifelong Christian, if I remember right. You know the God of the Bible. Many of the unchurched do not. As taught in public schools, moderns see only a one-dimensional world without a supernatural God, who has a final reckoning at the end of life. Yet many find that this one dimension of nature with nothing beyond is unsatisfying. They become curious about something more that will give deeper meaning to their lives. Few are really serious atheists, and a surprising many are curious about the supernatural. But they want to know what this "something more" means for them here and now. I am not downplaying the importance of eternal salvation. My point is that this isn't the lead question for most unchurched today. They are looking for present salvation.

John: Okay. I can see where you are coming from. But they need to know biblical truths.

Dave: Absolutely. They need to know the God of the Bible. For us such facts are the logical first step we learn to trust. Then comes the fruit of feelings the Spirit grows in believers. But the Spirit doesn't always follow our human logic. Often he keys off feelings and works curiosity about the faith that brings such feelings. That's why telling personal stories about encounters with the Spirit has become so much more important for Christian witness to the unbelieving world.

John: Okay. I follow your reasoning. But I don't know what to make out of your "present salvation." It is so different from what I learned in my previous Episcopalian experience.

Dave: In a moment I will offer an explanation for why the Reformers missed the concept that becomes so important today.

But first I want to share a conclusion by Gordon D. Fee, who has been a crucial guide for me in understanding salvation and the Spirit. He is today's foremost expert on the Holy Spirit in the letters of Paul and offers a detailed interpretation of each of the 143 passages where Paul referred to the Spirit. Significantly, the title of his study *is God's Empowering Presence.* Fee writes, "Salvation is in Christ, wrought by him through his death and resurrection; it is realized in the life of the believer [now] by the Holy Spirit, the empowering presence of God. Thus the presence of the Spirit is both the evidence that salvation has come, and the guarantee of our inheritance, of our sharing in the final glory of God through Christ."[49] Also he writes, "We miss both Paul's own life in Christ and his understanding of salvation if we do not see the central role the Spirit plays at every juncture."[50]

John: You are making a major claim when you suggest that Martin Luther and John Calvin didn't feature present salvation.

43

Dave: I suppose I am. Here is my reasoning. They weren't asking *why* be a Christian but rather *how* to be a true Christian. Not being a Christian wasn't an acceptable option in their ruler-dominated societies. As Christians become a minority in our American society, we need to face the prior question of *why*. What are the benefits? It is God the Spirit who delivers those benefits in this life.

Feelings

Ever since starting to focus on the fruit of the Spirit in preaching years ago, I have wondered why the desirable fruit of the Spirit haven't been more basic to the message of mainline churches. Such fruit certainly make the biblical message relevant to the listeners. The answer, I think, is that mainline intellectual heritage has been strongly biased against featuring emotions, which are regarded as unreliable. The strong bias is toward careful reasoning, separated from emotions, which are often irrational and damaging. But today we know that perceptions help shape emotions, and perceptions can be discussed and changed rationally. *Feeling* is a good word to describe an emotion subject to reason. *Affection* is an old-fashioned word that includes the will to act.

Suspicious of emotions, the Reformers didn't know what to make of heart conditions and so appealed to heads. When they talked about Christian living, they tended to focus on duty—what Christians should do. In that context fruit of the Spirit turned into virtues to be humanly pursued rather than Spirit-generated feelings to be enjoyed.

Rick: Are you claiming that Luther and Calvin were wrong?

Dave: No, but they were products of their age, pursuing questions of certainty rather than today's question of benefits. They saw the Spirit's job done with personal enlightenment as intellectual conviction. With this mindset they missed much of Paul's emphasis on the Spirit's role in daily living.

44

Rick: With your emphasis on emotions, are you saying we should become like Pentecostal churches? Once in a while, when I am channel surfing, I come across a show that seems even scary in its shallowness.

Dave: No, I am not advocating doing church like Pentecostals. For traditional Christians, reason remains very important, especially in mainline churches.

The proper question is, where do these feelings or affections come from? According to Paul, they come from the Spirit's touching and changing hearts of believers.

We can recapture Paul's approach by focusing on the key word he used to describe a Christian's special motivation and feelings. These are "gifts" the Spirit freely gives. The original word for "gift" is usually translated as "grace"—a gift freely given at the initiative of the giver. The big gift of eternal salvation is free, not earned by works. Additionally, special energy for church life is given at the initiative of the Spirit. Even the Christ-centered feelings of love, peace, and joy are freely given at the initiative of the Spirit.

John: I understand eternal salvation as a gift of grace. But how do you find more peace and joy if they have to be given at the initiative of the Spirit? What can I do about getting more? *Recognize the lack of, and humbly ask God! Eph. 3:20*

Dave: Good question. The short answer is that you put yourself where the Spirit can work on you. You expose yourself to God's word and do so in the company of other Christians who can share their insights and experiences. And come with the humility of a repentant heart. There is little room for the Spirit when you are full of yourself.

The most direct way is to ask the Father to send his Spirit. Jesus promised that the Father will always give the gift of that Spirit to all who ask. He said, "If earthly fathers know how to give good gifts to their children, how much more will your father in heaven give the Holy Spirit to those who ask him!"[51]

This promise leads to the next question. What gift would you most like the Spirit to work in your life right now? Eternal salvation you already have when you accept Christ as your Savior. We are talking now about present salvation.

Rick: Are you asking about what would make me really happy?

Dave: I suppose so. Let's use biblical language. What would make you feel blessed and full of joy?   *Eph. 4:16 fitly joined*

Rick: That's a tough question. You assume I have life all figured out. I would like to feel like I am a good person doing what I am supposed to do. Make that doing what God wants me to do. I would like good relationships with those around me, especially my family. I worry a lot about my job—whether I will be able to hang on to it and get promoted.

Amber: I would like to feel loved and do what I am supposed to do. I am worried about my children and whether I am being a good mother.

Amy: I'm single. Will I find a mate? Will we have children? I spend a lot of time feeling disappointed.

Dave: Let me see if I can put some labels on what you are looking for. You want to be a good person doing the right things. Paul's word for that is being "righteous," doing what God wants you to do. Having good relationships is a matter of loving and being loved. Less worry comes from trusting God more or having faith in God's providence. Put that all together, and we are talking about having hope for a good future. Such hope brings the peaceful feeling that your life is fitting together.

Can you see where I am headed? You want more of the big three: the love, faith, and hope Paul described as gifts the Spirit gives in 1 Corinthians 13. You also want more of what Paul called the righteousness, peace, and joy the Holy Spirit brings.[52]

Amber: *Love* is a tricky word. I think of it as a feeling. But I am learning it is also a rational choice. We talk about marriage as based on feelings of love. Yet I have been at it long enough to know that sometimes the feeling runs out, and you have to make a rational choice to submit to one another. Feelings really aren't reliable.

Dave: You are stating the issue well. We today need to learn that love is more than a feeling. It involves reasoned choices. For most of Western intellectual history, love was a rational choice to be attracted to something or someone. Emotions were downplayed. In earlier times their understanding that issuing a command to love someone made sense. It doesn't when you see love as an inner disposition, a feeling that comes from within, from the heart. By our understanding, you don't accomplish much when you try to tell someone else—a spouse, for instance—how to feel.

Reclaiming Paul's understanding is to recognize the power of the Spirit to actually produce feelings of love, joy, hope, trust, and the other fruit. They become a bonus, the present benefit of following Christ and seeking his Spirit. We can expect this because we base our faith on the facts of what Christ has done for us and the trust that he and the Father send their Spirit to us to be their presence in our daily lives.

The category of "fruit of the Spirit" appears in Paul's letter to the Galatians and therefore has received attention of scholars and preachers over the centuries. They and many preachers today see these qualities as virtues we are

---

to practice, and they then use them as a springboard for exhortations on living a more moral and Christlike life.

[margin note: Romans 7 — I find Not How to perform]

The fruit in effect become duties we should perform under our own powers. That would work if these were verbs describing behavior. But for Paul these fruit were nouns, describing conditions that lead to virtuous behavior. The feelings are prior to and shape behavior in relationships. Rather than duties, Paul saw the Spirit's fruit as opportunities for an enriched life in Christ.

When Paul wrote to the Thessalonians, Philippians, and Colossians, he described how their love, joy, and trust were growing, increasing, and overflowing. These are descriptions of what is happening rather than exhortations about what should happen.

Many theologians and preachers missed this distinction, I think, because they didn't see the Holy Spirit as an active agent changing hearts today. Thus while we confess Trinitarian beliefs, we in effect practice binitarian ministry, as if the Holy Spirit never made it out of the New Testament.

Engaging with God

John: As I asked earlier, how do you find more peace and joy if they have to be given at the initiative of the Spirit? How do we get more?

Dave: Paul would have answered by saying you should pray "that the Father [would] strengthen you with power through his Holy Spirit in your inner being."[53]

You can open the door to the Spirit and invite him in. Rooted in what you know about God's love, test how extravagant that love is. Welcome opportunities to stretch your trust. Experience how God provides for you in various situations. That's how to witness the power of the Spirit to quiet the fears that sap your energy, to lessen your worries, to surprise you with joy. Let the fullness of God in you help you live a full life.

What you can specifically do is to get better at recognizing encounters with the Spirit in your life. I previously described that you are looking for special feelings like peace, joy, awe, unity, or fresh energy that come as you experience, observe, or remember God's love working and Christ's grace healing. This might be the sense of satisfaction you get when you are giving special help to someone in the name of the Lord. Or it may be the special feeling of relief and peace you get remembering you are forgiven for something you wish you hadn't done.

Paul taught that Christians have two natures—the old natural, one that comes with being human, and the new nature shaped by the Spirit. You can observe for yourself when you are acting out your old nature and when you do something according to your spiritual nature. This is what Paul called living according to the flesh in contrast to living according to the Spirit in you. II CoR. 5; 16-21

Amy: What you are saying is that we should spend more time thinking about our feelings and motivations—whether we are acting according to our old sinful natures or according to our better natures in Christ.
Conscious, presence, awake

Dave: Call it Spirit awareness. You are really describing prayer, talking with God about what is going on in your life. At first, you might have to almost force yourself to spend time this way. But gradually the Spirit makes this discussion easier to carry on as your day progresses. I described his job as advocating what the Father and Son want in your life. With practice you get better at hearing his whispers and feeling his nudges.

Let me point out that the kind of prayer I am talking about, once it develops under the prodding of the Spirit, doesn't take much extra time. It is spontaneous conversation with God as your day goes along. But this happens best through regular exposure to the gospel message, which does take time. Think of it as an investment. Future salvation is already a gift you don't have to earn by regular church duty. But the benefits of present salvation increase and grow within you over time and with experience of the Spirit's work. The Spirit isn't under our control. But how we spend our time and prepare for the Spirit are decisions we make.

The Mystery of Kingdom Growth

Jesus consistently talked about the kingdom of God. How it grows in human hearts ultimately remains a mystery. It starts as a seed exposed to God's gospel message. Jesus explained how a seed planted in good soil can multiply thirty, sixty, or even one hundred times. Imagine what that would look like in your life. Basic to the analogy is that the kingdom of God's reign in our hearts is expected to grow. That is what seeds are supposed to do. We have been discussing what such growth looks like.

Jesus used a short parable to describe the underlying mystery: "A man went out to scatter his seed in the field. He sleeps at night, is up and about during the day, and all the while the seeds are sprouting and growing. Yet he does not know how it happens."[54]

As a farmer has to trust nature processes, so we have to trust God's spiritual processes worked through the Holy Spirit. We can't know the results God has in mind for each of us in this life. But we can trust his promise that through the Spirit's work the results will be good in this life, even if they aren't the ones we had in mind.

Another seed analogy describes how we can better prepare ourselves for the Spirit's work in us. Jesus told the parable of the seed, the sower, and the soil. Some soil was hard like a pathway, and the message about God's kingdom couldn't take root. The good soil was soft, and the seed produced a crop many times greater than what was sown.[55]

Think of the soil as our hearts. To cultivate means to break up the soil, to uproot weeds and let water seep deeper into the soil. I can cultivate the soil of my heart by recalling my shortcomings on the way to humbling myself before God and seeking the growth the Spirit wants to bring. Cultivating the soil of hearts can apply to whole congregations. Often their lives together harden into routines and low expectations so there is little room for the Spirit to generate new life. Cultivating the soil of our hearts is a good way to describe preparation for the Spirit.

So tell me, what is the condition of your heart right now? Are you still intent on pinning down exactly what you need to do to achieve the abundant life? Or is the burden getting lighter?

Sarah: I have to admit that this discussion is causing me to reflect on my life and marriage. I realize my shortcomings and have become more open to something new.

Dave: I think what you're saying qualifies as repentance, especially in your relationship with God and his expectations.

Sarah: I think of the times Bill, my husband, and I get into a standoff where I am disappointed in him and he lets me know his dissatisfaction with me, and then we argue. We are both learning to step back and calm down until we can talk about it more rationally later and remind ourselves of God's expectations.

Dave: Do you think that has anything to do with Christ's Spirit working more patience in both of you on the way to maturing your love?

51

Ministry as Planting, Watering and Cultivating,

We talked about the seed and the soil. Now let's focus on the sower in Jesus's parable. Paul very specifically took that identity for himself. The Corinthians were in conflict over preference for Apollos, a very good preacher, or Paul, who started the church there. Paul said he and Apollos were both only servants ("ministers" in Latin) for what God was doing. "I planted the seed, Apollos watered it, but God made it grow. So neither he who plants nor he who waters is anything, but only God, who makes it grow."[56] The "it" is the kingdom of God in individual hearts of those who come together in the local fellowship of the Holy Spirit.

"Church planter" has become a popular term in churches to describe someone who goes out to start a new congregation—a task that has become very difficult in current American society. But church planting can also happen in existing congregations, where leaders focus on building up a new level of fellowship or partnership among some of the participants. Ideally, this would happen among all, but realistically it needs to start with a few.

Paul described the work of spiritual leaders in a congregation. Kingdom growth happens differently in each believer. Besides planting seeds in some, they need to provide just the right amount of fertilizer and water for others in their various stages of growth, and they should be continually weeding and cultivating the soil.

This is a concept of ministry very different from a shepherd feeding and leading a flock of sheep who are all the same. We'll see more in Discussion 11.

Discussion Questions

1. How many of you can remember all the fruit of the Spirit Paul presented to the Galatians? Which would you like more of in your life?

2. Jesus said, "I have come that they may have life and have it to the full." Have you had this promise pointed out to you? What do you think Jesus meant? *Eph. 3:19*

3. What would make you feel especially blessed and full of joy? *Eph. 4:13-17*

4. How can you and I find more of God's promised peace and joy in our lives? *John 21:18-19* Yield + Follow only Jesus.

5. What do you think about the view that prayer is time we spend with God thinking about whether we are acting according to our old, sinful nature or according to our better nature in Christ?

Prayer without ceasing, is prayer as one breathes, It's constant and necessary - It's an underlying constant - exchange

Spirit - Reciprocation between God and each individual born of the Spirit...

It's growth as it increase nature the old nature passes to behold the New - II Cor. 5:16-21

9 fruits of the Spirit - Gal. 6:22-26

Love, Joy, peace, Kindness, gentleness, long suffering, Faith, meekness, Temperance

Discussion 5

Specially Motivated by the Spirit

The previous discussion focused on what Paul presented as the fruit of the Spirit—the changed insights and feelings that are basic to the abundant life in Christ. This discussion emphasizes the special motivation the Spirit arouses among members of a specific church fellowship for the common good. These spiritual gifts are the second layer of the cake of basic church life laid on the foundational layer of changes the Spirit brings to the hearts of believers. Both are usually treated as nice frosting rather than the basic cake itself.

Again, this exchange is among participants who are considering becoming partners for growth in the Spirit.

Dave: Where Christ's Spirit is at work among people, sharing God's word, he changes their understandings and feelings. As we discussed, his basic job is to enlighten, comfort, and advocate God's will in their lives. The Spirit also shapes our motivation for how we use our time and energy.

For this discussion we turn to what Paul described as the lesser gifts of the Spirit. The key explanation is in 1 Corinthians 12. He repeated this teaching in a broader context in Romans 12.

Let's talk about the motivation of each of us gathered here. What prompted you to commit to these sessions on growth in the Spirit? Compare that to your motivation for participating in church life five or ten years ago?

John: Good question. I have been asking myself why I am adding this extra obligation to a life that is already very busy. I suppose I am looking for something more in my life, some greater meaning.

Dave: If I remember right, you became a convinced Christian in college. Why?

John: I became involved with the InterVarsity Christian Fellowship at my state university. I liked what I saw among the other students, and I got a lot of encouragement. You asked about participating in this church. I became a regular when my wife and I recognized we needed to provide some kind of religious education for our first child after she was baptized here. It seems only fair that I should help with children's ministry. I couldn't think of a good reason to say no when I was asked to be on the finance committee.

Amber: I have always been involved in a church. That is the way I was raised. As I got older, I realized I needed to help, so I volunteer often. I know the church needs funds to operate, so I have learned to tithe. Why did I volunteer to become part of this group? I don't know. I guess I was curious.

Dave: You two cover much of the range of motivations I have seen in my twenty-five years of church ministry. Now let me ask you this: were you aware of the Holy Spirit's working on you from year to year?

Amber: Not really. I was just doing what seemed reasonable.

John: Sort of. But I thought I was just following through on becoming a better Christian.

Dave: What you were both doing is putting to use your special gifting by the Spirit to work for the common good of this local body of Christ. Paul's explanation to the Romans in chapter 12 is the simplest summary. Those Christians had different giftings for the various functions they performed as members of a congregation, a local body of Christ. There he listed preaching, teaching, serving, encouraging, contributing to the needs of others, as well as showing mercy and providing leadership. There is really nothing controversial here. All congregations would appreciate all those functions and the people who do them well.

Paul used the term "spiritual gift" in his first letter to the Corinthians, written several years earlier than Romans. He started chapter 12 with the statement "Now about spiritual gifts, brothers, I don't want you to be ignorant." His overall theme is diversity in a congregation. That he talked about motivation comes out in his explanation that it is the same God who is behind different kinds of gifts to do different kinds of ministry with different kinds of energy. Then he declared that each of the manifestations of the Spirit is given for the common good. That's why I can say that your motives for involvement in church life were manifestations of the Spirit.

Where this teaching gets controversial is in the listing Paul made to the Corinthians. Besides the routine functions he described to the Romans, here he also listed having miraculous powers, speaking in different kinds of tongues, and then interpreting those tongues. Historic church bodies haven't known what to make out of these "spectacular" giftings they wouldn't have honored, even if they had occurred. These examples and therefore this special work of the Spirit were ignored for most of church life after the first several generations in the first century until the twentieth century.

Ed: So what difference does it make to put the Holy Spirit label on what churches are already doing?

Differences in Motivation

Dave: The real issue is the importance of restoring Paul's perspective. I will answer that by sharing the conclusion I reached after visiting with forty or so pastors in my church body about ten years ago. I asked what their biggest problem was and therefore what help they wanted. The answer over and over again was that "we can't get anybody to do anything." My interpretation was that they were running out of energy, as reflected in declining attendance, contributions, and most obviously in filling all the committee positions they had.

Where will fresh energy for withering congregations in old church bodies come from? The only real source is the Holy Spirit. Traditional Protestant congregations don't seem to realize this.

Rick: I follow your reasoning, but why is it more important now than it was several generations ago?

Dave: I will answer that with my observation of what has happened to old-line congregations after the Second World War. The 1950s and '60s saw the great outmigration from the cities to the suburbs and the successful planting of many new churches. The first generation of suburbanites stayed loyal to their denomination. The new church plants set out to "recruit" new members. What attracted so many was the opportunity to find others looking for new attachments.

To make a long story short, many churches picked up a new vocabulary. They were looking for members who would "join" and tried to "involve" them in "activities" and "committees." Much church work revolved around "recruiting and caring" for "volunteers." None of these terms is historically connected to Christian churches. This is the language of social organizations, such as lodges and veterans groups that were also thriving at the time.

But this urge to join and form communities in America has declined significantly in recent decades. As a result, almost all traditional social organizations are withering, along with many congregations.

With that social club mentality, the motivation to participate in a congregation basically boils down to the argument that if you want the benefits, you have to contribute time and energy. Increasingly younger Americans are saying that the benefits aren't worth their effort. The benefits of committee work don't attract older participants much anymore either. Withering congregations face a fundamental issue of motivation for church life. Their accepted understandings no longer work.

Rick: So how does the Spirit work special motivation that would provide different results?

Dave: Let's go back to the many functions in the body Paul summarized for the Romans. The topic sentence for the section on different gifts in Romans 12 is the second verse: "Do not conform any longer to the pattern of this world, but be transformed by the renewing of your mind." For decades traditional churches drifted in their practices toward conforming their church life to the pattern of this world. It worked for a while. Now it doesn't in many congregations. Time to dig deeper.

Rick: *Transformation* is a big word these days that lots of organizations talk about. Would we just be conforming to some other pattern of this world?

Dave: Remember, Paul said it first, almost two thousand years ago. For him it was a very weighty concept. The original gives us the "metamorphosis" that we use to describe how a caterpillar turns into a butterfly. That is a fundamental change that is really beyond human ability alone. Such transformation of head and heart is what the Spirit specializes in. Paul really believed that the Spirit changes people's understandings and feelings. Part of that change is to work in believers a greater desire to love and serve others. We do well to stick to Paul's vocabulary. The word he used for service can properly be translated as "ministry." What he was really saying is that everyone in a congregation has a ministry to others, and these differ. Paul saw such ministry as an opportunity, not a duty.

So how do you know that what you're doing in a church is Spirit motivated? One sure sign is that you enjoy doing it. It seems to "fit" you. Another is that you get affirmation from others in the congregation that you do it well. Both are tied up in the concept of a gift from the Spirit. Such an opportunity is a gift to you, but it is also a gift to the congregation. If what you're doing builds up the fellowship, the Spirit is probably behind it.

Rick: But if a church waits for people to do only what they enjoy doing, a lot of church life wouldn't happen.

Dave: And this is what's happening in so many traditional congregations. That's why it is important to keep "volunteer" work embedded in the Spirit motivation.

All Do Spirit-Motivated Ministry

There is another problem traditional mainline congregations face. Our heritage makes a sharp distinction between clergy and laity. Clergy have special training and status. Laity are all the rest—the people. We tend to make the assumption that clergy do the real ministry and take care of the spiritual things (preaching, teaching the word, and celebrating the sacraments). The role of everybody else is to "pray, pay and support" this ministry. Of late, they need to also "volunteer" for special events. Clearly labeled second class, no wonder they don't do more in the church.

Take it from me. Paul didn't think in those terms. The

special status of clergy emerged when Christianity became the official religion of the Roman Empire and was reinforced through centuries of the medieval church practices that made clergy a special social class. We make too much out of *ordination*, a word used to translate Paul's sensible instruction to Titus to appoint elders in the congregations in Crete. He was all in favor of doing things "decently and in order" for the sake of peace in a congregation. Our version of the right and orderly way is to restrict clergy status only to those who have a college and graduate degree in theology. Whether those academic skills prepare for effective ministry and leadership in a congregation is increasingly questioned, especially now that so many mainline churches are withering away.

Rick: I'll have to admit I gave serious thought to studying for the ministry. But I just can't see how I could pull off moving the family and paying the bills for three years of seminary somewhere else.

Dave: Let me ask this. Have you taught others Bible lessons? Do you give encouragement to others in their Christian life? Can you see yourself preaching? Did you enjoy these experiences? Did you get positive feedback? If so, the Spirit may be preparing you for the ministry pastors do. It should be our job as a church to bring necessary preparation here to you rather than to separate you from a congregation and send you off to the very different culture of a seminary. Increasingly, robust congregations are heading in this direction, much to the frustration of many seminaries.

Who does the real ministry in a congregation? This is the key to motivation. Are the specially trained and ordained the only ones who do ministry? Or can and should everyone do real ministry? The mainline tradition is that spiritual matters and real ministry are delegated to the ordained, with the rest helping but mostly being receivers of ministry. Among evangelicals and Pentecostals, ministry is something everyone does under the leadership of a pastor they have confidence in. They take the priesthood of all believers very seriously.

In our English tradition from earlier centuries, *minister* came to describe high-status clergy, and "ministry" is what a minister of religion does. In fact, for tax purposes, the Internal Revenue Service today uses the technical term "minister of religion" to describe someone a church body has ordained or commissioned. "The ministry" is what I decided to study for back in high school

But Paul simply didn't think in terms of this lofty status. The word he used gives us "deacon," and in Greek it means "a servant" or "to serve," which was low-status work. The Latin equivalent is "to minister or do ministry," from the same root that gives us minus or minor—lesser. That originally described low-status work. But over time it was also used for the minister/servant of the king, and that was very high status, like being a prime minister in a government. The King James translation consistently used "minister" for the servant Paul had in mind. The Revised Standard Version (1952) still mostly used "minister." Finally, the New International Version (1973) consistently uses "servant," which is closer to what Paul meant. For Paul all the saints gathered as a church are servants. The job of church leaders is to prepare God's people for works of service—that is, for ministry—so that the body of Christ may be built up.[57]

The bottom line to all these translation problems is that when you are involved in helping God's love work and Christ's grace heal, you are doing real ministry.

The kind of special motivation by the Spirit I am featuring raises basic questions about whether a congregation's way of doing things presents barriers to what the Spirit would like to accomplish among those people. Organizational procedures can become barriers, especially in congregations that are overly organized. For Paul the congregation was the informal fellowship of the Holy Spirit, not the formalized organization developed to protect and shape the fellowship. *agenda based*

John: Are you suggesting that Spirit-motivated church work can change how we organize a congregation?

Dave: Probably. This is a big topic. For now I will just observe that many of the present forms of the institutional church may well wither away in coming decades. This could be healthy, if you remember that the real church is the informal fellowship of the Holy Spirit that takes on organizational forms to accomplish its work. The challenge will be to develop better organizational ways that support rather than to become a barrier to the Spirit's work.

A Strange Predicament for Traditional Churches

Here are a few more perspectives on the plight of mainline churches. As I said, our heritage is that spiritual matters were delegated to the special class of clergy, and whatever the laity did was almost by definition not spiritual. That worked fine for centuries when most people lived all their lives in very stable rural settings. Churches were "parishes," a geographic term for all the people living in the village or small town. There are good sociological reasons for the institutional church forms that emerged in the sixteenth to nineteenth centuries. But of course in the early twentieth century, huge numbers of people left the farm to move to the cities, and then in the second half of that century, many moved out of the central cities to the suburbs. About 85 percent of the American population lived in rural and small towns; now fewer than 15 percent do. The assumptions of old-style parish ministry simply don't fit most churches anymore.

When newly planted suburban churches had to work at attracting new members, they turned to the well-known model of social organizations that were thriving around them. These practices worked for decades, and God's kingdom advanced in many lives. But the approaches of this model no longer work with younger generations.

So mainline churches find themselves in a strange predicament in the twenty-first century. Their heritage leaves them with participants who are passive in spiritual matters in a context that barely recognizes the Holy Spirit as a special force. To activate members, most congregations turned to the model of social organizations, which of course don't recognize any spiritual energy. Meanwhile many evangelical churches seem to be doing better at reaching people. Most are from a "free" church background, separate from state-sponsored mainline churches. They don't assume the strong clergy/laity distinction, and many participants are quite comfortable doing spiritual activities, such as witnessing to their faith. Meanwhile Pentecostal churches are faring the best throughout the world, but their emotional focus on the Spirit's gifts doesn't fit well with the more rational approach of churches that are strongly oriented to the word.

I offer this summary as a way to highlight the direction forward for withering churches. We need to become more comfortable working with the special gifts of the Spirit. Call it a strategy, if you will.

Amy: Maybe that seems obvious to you, but it doesn't to me. I am not used to thinking about village church settings or comparing a church to a social organization and its volunteers. Can't we just talk about our church?

Dave: Yes, I'm sorry. We do want to talk about our church. Here are two thoughts in response to your concern.

What I have done is slip into the role of a business school professor, which I used to be, teaching a strategy course, which I used to do. Analyze the situation and recommend next steps.

The situation mainline churches face is complicated. What worked for centuries is no longer so effective. The reason is that the society we face is changing. Understanding those changes makes it easier to figure out how churches can respond to become effective again. Churches, too, can benefit from basic reasoning about how to be effective in a new social environment.

Actually most churches resist thinking in terms of psychological and sociological insights I am offering because such "worldly" approaches don't seem sufficiently spiritual; churches are supposed to be special. I agree that churches need to be different. But increasingly they are not. The theological challenge is to be more precise about what makes churches different from other human enterprises. I think the answer is dependence on the Holy Spirit.

Frank: I, too, am struggling. I suppose what you want us to say is that congregations should learn how to recognize and talk about the Holy Spirit.

Dave: Yes, thank you. Mainline and many Baptist churches are highly focused on the objectively true word of God in the scriptures, as well they should be. But as I have suggested, they don't know what to make out of the unpredictable third person of the Trinity and the subjective feelings he brings. For most, the Holy Spirit isn't a living, active presence. That is why I think the major challenge facing these churches is to name and share encounters with Christ's Spirit and to seek more. This is the subtitle of my book on *Your Encounters with the Holy Spirit: Name and Share Them—Seek More*. We are talking about the naming stage now—recognizing the Spirit's work. You can see fresh energy emerging among those who share their encounters

Jim: If I remember right, your definition told us to look for the Spirit in situations that bring better understanding of God's ways and special feelings, such as peace, joy, or fresh energy.

Dave: Yes. And you will have increased confidence when better understanding and special feelings happen in the context of God's love working and Christ's grace healing. As Jesus said, "The Advocate will bring glory to me by taking from what is mine and making it known to you." The gospel is all about God's love in sending his Son into our world and what Jesus Christ in his life, death, and resurrection accomplished for us. Christ's Spirit is now his agent for carrying forward and accomplishing God's work in our lives today.

Ministry as Coaching

The emphasis on motivation in this discussion brings to mind specialists in motivation today. My PhD is in organizational behavior, which focuses on performance and satisfaction in workplaces. Of late this specialty has morphed into sports psychology, the study of peak performance for athletes. Team coaches are the hands-on practitioners for obtaining peak performance from individual athletes and then especially from the whole team. Technically no one can motivate someone else. This movement has to come from within the person. But coaches can shape the motivation present in an athlete by showing ways and arranging opportunities for him or her to perform as well as possible. Good coaches get to know their athletes very well.

Paul thought like a coach when he considered the variety of giftings by the Spirit present among all in a congregation. We know he liked sports and used sports analogies, such as running the race, boxing, and pummeling the body into submission. But Greeks and Romans focused on individual competitions, such as racing and boxing, and didn't take team competitions seriously. If they had, I think Paul would have used that analogy of coach for the ministry of helping individuals within a congregation reach their peak performance for the common good. Paul thought like a coach. Church leaders can do so, too.

Here's what I would like to discuss next time. We need to address the concept of a personal spiritual journey. That phrase is typically not in mainline church vocabulary, because in the old parish framework, most members were assumed to be passive and like everyone else. There was resistance to some becoming different from others.

Underlying a believer's spiritual journey is Paul's focus on growth in the Spirit. It is built into the concept of fruit grown by the Spirit. Growth is also built into the concept of finding and making better use of what the Spirit is gifting you to do. A couple of decades ago, many Protestant congregations were involved in discussions of church growth. That was mostly quantitative growth in numbers, something beyond human endeavor alone. Here we need to talk about qualitative growth, such as the changes the Spirit brings into individual lives.

This discussion finishes Part 2 on recognizing how the Spirit works today. The next four discussions address how to grow in the Spirit's influence on your life.

Discussion Questions

1. What is your motivation, reader, for investing your efforts in exploring fresh energy for your spiritual life?
2. How would you describe the energy level of most participants in your congregation—low motivation, high motivation, or somewhere in between?
3. Paul wrote in Romans 12: 2, "Do not conform any longer to the pattern of this world, but be transformed

by the renewing of your mind." What are your thoughts on how this would happen?

4. Who does ministry in your congregation?
5. What makes a church different from other social organizations?

Part 3: Growing in the Spirit

Discussion 6

Recognizing Growth in the Spirit

Peter, the apostle, used an intriguing phrase to end his second letter: "Grow in the grace and knowledge of our Lord and Savior Jesus Christ."[58]

To grow in knowledge is something most of us now continually do to be productive in a fast-changing world, and learning such skills seems to come naturally to those who want the benefit of such knowledge. Here Peter meant to grow in the knowledge of God's ways with humans, as described in scripture. That is a lifelong process.

But how to do you grow in grace? In our heritage we seldom ask this question. Such growth, too, is a lifelong process. Under the power of the Spirit, it, too, can come naturally.

We return to the participants discussing spiritual growth.

Dave: To grow in grace is to grow in the Holy Spirit. More specifically, it is to grow in the gifts of the Spirit.

Let's talk about what growth in Christ's Spirit looks like. Think beyond the experiences of a new Christian or follower of Christ awakened to a new understanding. Those can be dramatic stories. I want you to think about church people who have been walking with the Spirit for years. What is distinctive about them?

Amber: I think of my grandmother. She always seemed calm and collected. She took an active interest in the lives of those around her. She had a hard early life in the Depression, but I had the feeling this made her stronger. I saw how important her daily devotion was, and she would often share insights that came to her.

Dave: I suspect I know the answer to this question. Did she gossip a lot?

Amber: No, now that you mention it. She always had a kind word for everyone. For me she had kind of an "aura" about her.

John: My image is of the young InterVarsity leader who helped me come to faith in college. I knew he had wrestled with the same issues that concerned me. He always had time. I learned that he had to raise his own support. He and his wife had to be very careful with their dollars, and yet they were raising three children.

Sarah: I am impressed with a young mother I see here at church. She has five children, from a baby to an eighth-grader. She is just always so patient and calm. I have been in a group with her, and I know how deep her faith is. It's got to be a hectic life with all those kids. Yet she always seems to have a smile. I'd love to have that kind of patience.

Dave: Let me tell you about my colleague in ministry when I was the administrative pastor. He clearly was the spiritual leader. Many others and I were impressed that on the first Monday of the month, he would go off to a local monastery to pray. He would take church statistics and reports with him, and by the afternoon he was praying for guidance in discerning God's will for the congregation. He had a knack for identifying and committing to new ministry initiatives with the confidence that they would be supported by additional offerings to cover them. And supported they were by the end of that year.

The question I want us to focus on in this discussion is, how do you recognize when a believer has grown in the Spirit? What kind of growth should we expect in Christians who have been living for years in a relationship with Jesus Christ?

Your grandmother, Amber, has a special peace and has remarkable goodness in relationships with others. John, your InterVarsity friend, seems to have a gentleness with others and a spirit of self-sacrificial service. Sarah, do you think the young mother's patience has anything to do with her faith? I know that my colleague has special discernment and wisdom in anticipating where the Spirit was leading.

These examples are of committed Christians. Do you think their unusual spirit and behavior comes only from natural temperament? Were they created that way? Or did they grow over time into the fuller maturity their lives demonstrate? Such growth is our topic here. But temperament is important, too. There is much to learn about how the Spirit can work best when he encounters us in ways that fit our spiritual temperaments. This is the topic of Discussion 9, which comes later.

Growth into greater Christian maturity is the Spirit's specialty. We are looking primarily for the impact the Spirit has on feelings and motivation, and how deep rooted these have become. When the Spirit is at work, he moves us beyond head knowledge to conditions of the heart. Out of changed hearts come the behaviors that are God pleasing. We are looking for what happens "because God has poured out his love into our hearts by the Holy Spirit."[59]

God's Gifts for His People

Consider this statement of Paul: "We have different gifts, according to the grace given us."[60] The word *grace* we think we know because it is so basic to the gospel. In the original it is *charis*—God's favor freely given and not earned. This is the favor most basically given in God's merciful acceptance of Christ's redemption earned for each of us. This favor continues in his attitude to his followers today. The word *charis* is from the viewpoint of the giver.

From the viewpoint of the receiver, *charis* becomes *charisma*, the plural of which is *charismata*. In Paul's use, the gifts (plural) are received from the Spirit—namely special motivation to serve and also feelings like love, peace, and patience produced by the Spirit. So we have the major gift of God's basic favor to his people in Christ and then his more routine gifts to his people through the Spirit. Both are the result of God's favor—his grace.

We gain a key insight from those original words of God's *charis* and the Spirit's *charismata*. The root word behind both is *chara*, which simply means "joy." God's intent for his gift of Christ is to bring us joy. The Holy Spirit works such joy into our hearts. Joy cannot be commanded or required. It is a feeling that arises within a person, a sense of contented pleasure with our circumstances. Such "happiness," to adapt the current word, has little to do with material circumstances. Being right with God and his blessings brings the highest joy. Even or especially in tragedy, such joy can express the peace of feeling "It Is Well with My Soul."

Consider one more variation on the word *charis*. Put *eu* in front of it, and we have the Greek word for "thanksgiving," *eucharistia*. Joy blends into giving thanks for the sources of that joy. According to one New Testament scholar's count, joy and thanksgiving are the two most frequently expressed or encouraged emotions in the New Testament.[61] They describe emotional fullness, the abundant life Jesus came to give. We can recognize such heightened emotions as expressions of present salvation.

This word group points us toward how to recognize growth in the Spirit. In the context of Christian living, look for changes happening in yourself and others. Look for increased understanding and readiness to serve others. Look for a heart condition showing more fruit of the Spirit, such as love, joy, and peace. These are the gifts of the Spirit.

Growing in grace isn't something we do. It happens to us. We discover it growing in us, like the seed of God's reign in hearts. His seeds need to be planted and watered. But God gives the growth.[62] Growth of God's reign in the hearts of his people isn't man made. The Spirit gives or produces it.

Growing in Joy, Love, and Trust

We can gain confidence in Paul's understanding of growth by considering the passages where he recognized that growth has happened among believers. When he used such words and phrases as "increased," "overflowing," and "growing more and more," what did he see?

- He told the Philippians that he would like to remain with them "for your *progress* and *joy* in the faith, so that through my being with you again your *joy* in Christ Jesus will *overflow* on account of me" (emphasis added).[63]
- He prayed that the Lord would make the Thessalonians' love "*increase and overflow* for each other and for everyone else" (emphasis added).[64]
- In his second letter to them, he thanked God that the Thessalonians' faith was growing more and more, and that the love every one of them had for each other was increasing.[65]
- Paul's prayer to the Philippians was that their love would abound more and more in knowledge and depth of insight so they could discern what was best.[66] Here it is not knowledge that produces love but love that

shapes knowledge. *Discernment* is a good word for what happens under the Spirit's influence.

- Paul was thankful that the Thessalonians welcomed his message with *joy* the Holy Spirit gave.[67] He thanked God that the Colossians' faith and love would spring from the hope they had heard about in the word of truth, the gospel, which was bearing fruit and growing all over the world."[68]

Ed: Okay. I get that through the Spirit we are supposed to grow in love and faith. I have heard that all my life. I know in my head that God is love, and we are supposed to love him.

Dave: How that happens is key here. Love is complicated. So let's rather focus on the joy Paul emphasized. Even according to the dictionary, joy is an emotion that rises up from within. Joy is a key characteristic that emerges from the Spirit's work, according to Paul. He told the Romans that living in the kingdom of God is a matter of righteousness, peace, and *joy* in the Holy Spirit.[69] He wished that the God of hope would fill them with all *joy* and peace.[70] He commended the Philippians that despite their poverty, their overflowing *joy* yielded a generous contribution.[71]

John: It is surprising to see such prominence of joy in this listing. Many individual Christians and their congregations don't give the impression of being full of joy. I grew up thinking that church is a very somber place. It's not where you go to have fun.

Dave: Your comment, John, is a good reason to point out that Paul's emphasis on fruit of the spirit wasn't the direction the Reformers took in explaining the work of the Holy Spirit. The larger category of gifts of the Spirit in 1 Corinthians 12 and Galatians 5 simply didn't receive much attention in their writings and teachings.

Let me review a little history here so you can better appreciate a renewed emphasis on Paul's understanding of gifts of the Spirit in church life today.

I have talked about the two-sided coin we make available in our church. On one side is an imprinted cross. On the other side is the image of a dove. Sometimes in his writing Paul featured the cross-Christ perspective, and other times it was the dove-Spirit perspective.

The Reformers, however, stayed focused on the Christ side, the full meaning of which was their major rediscovery. Paul referred to Christ 360 times in his writings. He was truly Christocentric. His whole thinking revolved around the decisive change in our relationship with God because of what Jesus Christ did in the past in his life, death, and resurrection. Now everyone who accepts Christ has a new status in God's sight. Paul's phrase for that condition is being "in Christ" and thus reclaimed for God's greater purposes in life.

But the Reformers' assumption made recognition of the full meaning of the dove-Spirit side difficult. For them the major issue was the relationship between justification and sanctification. The work of Christ is justification—to make us righteous or just before God. For them featured work of the Spirit is sanctification—to make us holy or pure, which is the meaning of *sanctus*. Belief in the Spirit, in Luther's catechism explanation, is to acknowledge that the Spirit has called me by the gospel, enlightened me with his gifts, and sanctified and kept me in the true faith. The Spirit is there in the background, bringing about these important results in the life of Christians. Gal. 2:20 + 6:12-15

But focusing on sanctification makes it hard to get specific about how the Spirit does his work, especially in churches where saving faith is initiated with the baptism of infants. Gifts of the Spirit are acknowledged but only in reference to enlightened understanding, reflecting the Reformers' emphasis on head knowledge. There is no reference to internal, heartfelt changes produced by the Spirit, as Paul's focus on fruit of the Spirit emphasized.

[margin handwriting: yield to fruit]

The "sanctification" process could be interpreted to include internal changes. But the process of "making holy" tends to get measured in good works—the more holy you get, the more good works you do. Then the emphasis is back on our behavior. Then we too readily slip into thinking that our holy behavior is what makes us right with God. By then we too easily have lost perspective on Paul's central teaching that we are saved by grace; it is the gift of God, not by works so no one can boast.[72] Finding certainty in God's grace is the central discovery of the Reformation.

[margin handwriting: inner working vs. work of the flesh out of Word Acts!]

But associating the Spirit with sanctification can produce some strange results. In the late nineteenth century, there was a strong Protestant holiness movement that started in England and spread over to America. The central premise was that in Christ we are new people, and that means holy people. In this view, since in conversion we become fully holy, church life tends to revolve around being vigilant for unholy behaviors that need to be corrected. While there was much to celebrate in being converted, the daily life too often became the grim process of intimidating those who fell short. This approach produced much of the "holier than thou" attitude so many found offensive, especially the unchurched. *Woe Isa. 65:5*

John: Count me among those who resist Christians who convey moral superiority. I learned the hard way that my friends get uncomfortable with talk of holiness.

Dave: Then we are on the same page. I don't think holiness or sanctification is the best category for understanding the work of the Spirit. He works on changing hearts of believers. From changed hearts come new motivations to behave in better ways in our relationships with God and others. More important than the behavior is the motivation. The fruit of the Spirit's work within a believer is ever-increasing love, joy, peace, patience, kindness, gentleness, and self-control, which then motivate changed behavior. Paul also talks about being transformed by the renewal of our minds. Such inward change in a believer's thinking, disposition, and attitude is the core of what happens on the Christ's Spirit side of the coin of God's presence today.

While holiness is a key characteristic in the Old Testament, it was no longer a major part of Paul's understanding of the new covenant. In deference to his Jewish audience, he wrote about the end result of being holy and acceptable through Christ's redemption. But in only twelve places did he recognize sanctification as a process, and in only two of those did he identify the process as the work of the Spirit.[73] Compare that to the hundreds of times he wrote about love, joy, peace, hope, patience, and other fruit of the Spirit; and increased motivation to serve.

To grow in the Spirit is to grow into a new nature characterized by changed perceptions, attitudes, and feelings. The Spirit's fruit are primarily predispositions, not whatever virtuous behavior flows from them. To recognize the Spirit at work, look for changed thinking and emerging godly heart conditions or feelings. Thriving in the Spirit is most visible in lives that reflect joy, peace, and love.

Sarah: Are you sure feelings are so important? I thought we weren't supposed to look to our feelings for assurance of God's grace in our lives.

Dave: True. The constant challenge is to keep personal feelings in the right sequence in our relationship to God. It has to start with the *facts* conveyed in scripture—that God looks favorably on all people because of their redemption through Jesus Christ. All who believe this promise are his. Then comes the personal act of trust or *faith* in this promise. Out of such trust come the right kind of Spirit-shaped *feelings* we have been talking about. The sequence is fact, faith, feelings. Such feelings we should celebrate.

Paul expressed the right sequence in his encouragement to the Colossians: "Just as you received Christ Jesus as Lord, continue to live in him, rooted and built up in him, strengthened in the faith you were taught and overflowing with thanksgiving."[74] The faith that accepts Christ as Lord is different from the faith or trust in God's providence that can be strengthened for daily living. Such trust can become more deeply rooted as well as built up. The first kind of accepting faith is certainly worked by the Spirit. The second kind of faith or trust that can be increased and better rooted is also a gift of the Spirit and gives us more to talk about.

Historically mainline churches have had low expectations for such Spirit-gifted growth to be continued over the years. For children we do all accept the responsibility to teach children the basic knowledge of the Christian faith into which they were baptized as infants. But for all practical purposes, once confirmed, they are considered to be set for the rest of their lives as Christians, usually with low expectations of more spiritual growth later.

This approach could work well in communities where everyone believed the same thing and the common faith wasn't challenged. It continued to work into the twentieth century when mainline churches represented the public religion in America and the basics of the faith weren't seriously challenged. The story of the now forty year decline

David S. Luecke

of mainline church bodies reveals that the faith of so many of its members wasn't well rooted, and they fell away when confronted with the different beliefs and lives of so many others in a changing American culture. *matt. 24:10-13*
Hebrews 6: 4-6

The fundamental challenge facing mainline churches today is to foster participants' ongoing growth upward in the fruit of the Spirit and downward into deeper roots. The best means to that goal is to renew Paul's emphasis on the inward, heart-changing gifts of the Holy Spirit that produce growth in the Christian's life.

Discussion Questions

1. How do you recognize when someone has grown in the Spirit? *Not easily provoked.*
2. When you hear the song "Amazing Grace," what is your understanding of God's grace? *Amazing!*
3. Are you making progress in your Christian life? Paul coupled that with greater joy. Are you making progress in your joy? *upward levels ↑ II Cor. 3:18*
4. Growing in faith means to grow in trusting someone or something. Have you grown in the trust you place in someone, like a child or a friend? Have you grown in trusting God?
5. How would you describe your personal spiritual journey in your life so far?

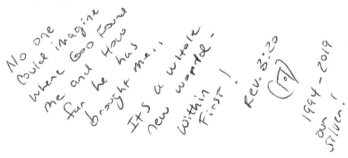

78

Discussion 7

Personal Growth Journeys Shaped by the Spirit

Right after Paul gave his sample listing of fruit of the Spirit, he offered the Galatians this challenge: "Since we live by the Spirit, let us keep in step with the Spirit."[75] To walk with the Spirit through the personal circumstances of life over weeks and years amounts to a personal spiritual journey. By God's grace, we have the opportunity to grow closer to God as we experience the Spirit's gifts.

The ministry heritage of church bodies shaped by the Reformation excels at bringing comfort to their people in times of difficulty. Basic to the gospel is the assurance of forgiveness of sins and eternity with God. But the tradition doesn't do well in highlighting expectations of a believer's personal movement or growth in faith. Beyond times of grief, there is little reflection on a member's changing inward heart condition.

Paying more attention to a believer's spiritual journey would be a worthwhile shift in the ministry of traditional churches. The heritage features the objective biblical truth of the gospel and the constant encouragement to rely on God's love and Christ's grace. This is the right sequence of fact and faith. But the next step of personal feelings about these truths is left largely unexplored and undeveloped. Recovering Paul's emphasis on the gifts of the Spirit, especially the fruit, would provide a biblical vocabulary to assess and share personal feelings.

When the purpose of church life is to grow in the fruit of love, joy, hope, and peace, "going to church" becomes more than doing a duty. Gathering with other believers and sharing spiritual journeys become an opportunity. Instead of church life remaining mostly a habit, Christians can look forward to experiencing more hope, joy, and peace in the future. Call this the opportunity to thrive in the faith. The Holy Spirit has always been producing these changes in believers. He can do so better when we regularly look and ask for his influence.

Let's go back to discussion with the participants who are partners in GROWTH of the Spirit.

Dave: Last time we talked about people you know who seemed to have a distinctive walk with the Spirit over the years—Amber's saintly grandmother, John's campus ministry friend, Sarah's recall of a busy but patient mother, and my experience with a spiritual pastor who seemed very close to God. How would you describe yourself at your present stage of growth? Let's stay with the sense of being close to God or far from God.

John, before you had your college experience with your friend and the Christian fellowship he led, would you describe yourself as far from God?

John: Sure. I didn't even think about God. So I was far away.

Dave: Your college experience brought you closer to God. How did that feel?

John: I felt a stronger sense of purpose. I felt relief that God would provide for me. I felt accepted by friends who cared for me.

Dave: Do you still feel that way today?

John: Sort of but not as much. Those were special times. My life has gotten very busy. I guess I am here because I want to recapture some of that feeling.

Dave: Sarah, in a previous discussion about the abundant life in Jesus, you said that for you such a life would overflow with love. What are you thinking now that we have focused on the Spirit's gift of love along with the other fruit?

Sarah: I'm here for more. It is new to me that I can ask the Father to send his Spirit to change my heart so that I am more loving. Makes sense.

Dave: Amber, in a previous discussion you said your confirmation was very important to you. I assume you felt close to God then? Have you always felt the same way?

Amber: No, high school was tough, and I wasn't so sure of myself then. Getting back into the routine of church life with my family has helped.

Dave: Do you look forward to feeling closer to God? Does thriving in the Spirit seem like a good thing for you?

Amber: Sure. But I don't know what that means yet. My life is pretty busy now. I don't want to add another responsibility.

Dave: I hope by the time we are done that thriving in the Spirit will seem exciting enough to you to find opportunities to name and share your encounters.

What I have been doing is probing into the personal journey of some of you. A spiritual journey is simply the story of a Christian's relationship with Jesus Christ over the years of his or her life. Were there any high points that seem memorable? Were there times when they were drifting away from church and when their faith didn't seem important?

Even when talking with very traditional mainline Christians, I can almost always find a time when the faith took on more meaning to them, perhaps at the death of someone close, and also after years when faith and church weren't a high priority. Some think in terms of mountaintop experiences they might have had. Hearing these stories is one of the joys of ministry for me. I like to challenge them to work out for themselves what might have led to this awakening experience, as small as it might be, and to become aware of what might aid further growth.

Some churchgoers have dramatic stories. These I enjoy because they can put me in awe of the power of the Spirit. Telling these stories can be very encouraging to others, giving them perhaps a sense of hope for their relationship with Christ.

Paul encouraged Christ's followers to keep in step with the Spirit. Walking with the Spirit is a great focus for daily living. A constant question can be, where is the Spirit leading me today? What should I be doing in this specific situation?

Here is a chart I like to work with. On the vertical left side is the dimension of experiences when you felt close to God and other times when you felt farther away. The bottom line invites you to remember your age at that point—whether you were a child, teen, young adult, or in the middle of your life and now, whatever your age.

Accept the challenge to recall when in your life you felt close to or far from God. You may well have a jagged line with ups and downs. Here is a chart of a hypothetical journey for someone who grew up in a traditional curch family.

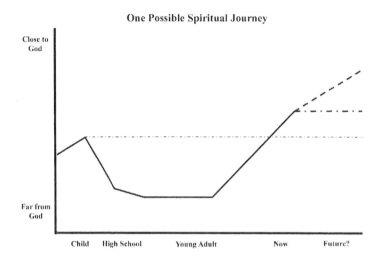

One Possible Spiritual Journey

From this believer's earliest memories, Jesus was important to her. She felt especially close to him at her confirmation service at the end of the eighth grade. Then came high school when her faith was challenged, followed by experiencing further confusion in college and getting her own life started. She was at a low point in her relationship with God as a young adult. Making the vows of a church wedding pulled her closer to God. Then the young marrieds had lots of things to learn and do on their own when God didn't seem so important. When their children got to school age, they thought more about church and God for the sake of the children. The dotted line at the end of the graph projects the rest of their personal spiritual journey. Will they be drawn closer to God, stay flat, or even drift farther away?

The small dotted line that starts at confirmation and continues flat to the present is the kind of journey our traditions project. Once confirmed, all you need to do is stay faithful. There is no vocabulary for being drawn closer or falling farther away. We all know such movement up or down happens, but we don't know how to talk about it beyond noting superficially that John Doe has fallen away from the church.

Where to go from here is the issue at hand for believers regardless of age. My purpose in these discussions is to describe the benefits of a closer relationship with God. To thrive in Christ's Spirit is to grow in enjoyment of his gifts, especially fruit like love, peace, hope, and patience. Whatever your age and condition in life, God has more good things in store for your abundant life in Christ. There are two dotted lines into the future on this chart. Will you be drawn closer to God, or do you expect your future faith life to be the same as it is now?

A spiritual journey chart like the one above wasn't important in a traditional church in a small town setting where everybody had about the same experiences through life. Many would consider a flat line from confirmation on through the years to death as ideal. The goal would be to keep the sheep from wandering off and getting lost.

Two major shifts have happened since the days of traditional churches in traditional settings. One is the collapse of the Sunday school movement several decades ago. Now a vast majority of high school kids have had little exposure to biblical stories and teachings. Test it out for yourself. In other than a church setting, ask a teen about a well-known biblical story, such as David and Jonathan or the child Jesus in the temple, and see what kind of response you get.

The second shift is the loss of loyalty to church bodies and their congregations. Statistically, most adults are no longer churched. If and when they would consider "going to church," their main question would be, what are the benefits for me? Eternal salvation is no longer a driving concern for most. Greater exposure to the Spirit and the gifts he brings is rightfully one of the benefits of being a Christian.

Amber: Your line chart comes close to describing my spiritual journey. Confirmation was a very important event in my life. But I have often thought I'm inadequately prepared for the kind of busy life I lead. I know I should do more Bible study, but I can't find time.

Rick: Your emphasis on the Spirit's growing his fruit in our lives sounds fine. But it also seems much too easy. Surely we have to work at it. I know I need to be a better disciple, and I feel guilty that I don't do more of what a disciple should do. That's not easy for me.

Dave: Perhaps you have a misunderstanding of discipleship.

John: You make spiritual growth sound easy. From what little I have heard, I thought it was hard work with a lot exercises and disciplines to do.

Dave: Yes, there is a long tradition of something called "spiritual formation," which is mostly focused on what spiritual masters have done and written over the centuries. They make it seem hard, or at least beyond what ordinary Christians would do. Frankly, I find much of that off putting and embedded in a Roman Catholic tradition not focused on grace and God's free gifts. My goal is to help you grow in the Spirit in ways that come most naturally. That has a lot to do with personal temperaments I will talk about in Discussion 9.

God really wants to give the Spirit's gifts to his people and to you in particular. Some Christians learn to see God as stingy, giving only what we earn. Paul experienced and taught that God wants to be generous and give his gifts freely. We can receive them better when we know what we're looking for, especially when we let others help us to see.

Consider this claim, which Gary Thomas well stated: "Not a second of our existence passes without God thinking about how to turn our hearts toward him. The almost unbelievable joy is that you can develop a relationship with God that he will have with no one else. God eagerly, passionately, yearns for that relationship. He is just as eager to love and know you as he was to know Moses, David, and Mary. You are no less precious to him than were those heroes of the faith."[76]

A key part to such a relationship is a readiness to seek the Spirit's gifts from God, whom we recognize as close at hand. This looks like a personal consciousness that God is constantly trying to break through to us with his gifts. Think of the image at the end of Revelation 3 of Christ's Spirit knocking on the door. "If anyone hears my voice and opens the door, I will come in and eat with him." Those who open the door, even a crack, are the people of God to whom the gifts of God will come. Such asking amounts to prayer. Jesus taught that the Father will always send the Spirit to those who ask.[77]

Stages of Growth

Sarah: Is there any way to describe at what stage of growth in the Spirit a believer is at a specific time of his or her life?

Dave: Yes, I can offer several. One is by psychologist James Fowler.[78] He distinguishes six stages, but for our purposes, the first four are important.

Stage 1: Literal view of God	God is like Daddy.
Stage 2: What's fair is fair.	You get from God what you earn.
Stage 3: I believe what the church teaches.	Confirmation
Stage 4: As I see it, God is ...	Knowledge turns into heartfelt conviction.

The first stage is that of a small child who takes everything literally. When he or she hears about God the Father, the child can think of only his or her own daddy.

The second stage is that of about a ten-year-old who is preoccupied with fairness. "That's not fair" is a frequent complaint. Many stay stuck at that stage through their adulthood, constantly assuming they have to earn God's favor. They may talk about grace, but they don't understand it.

The third stage is represented by a fourteen-year-old at confirmation. He or she know catechism answers, which used to be enough to get through life in a predominantly Christian community.

The fourth stage comes from having those answers challenged through struggles, perhaps in high school or college. Many never recover and drift away. Those who receive good guidance can find their way back to Christian faith and are stronger for the struggle. Their head knowledge has turned into heartfelt conviction. In today's world, it is wise to alert confirmands about the struggles ahead and regularly hear testimony from those who are a few years older, those who have become stronger in their faith through their struggles.

The other framework comes from Martin Luther in an early sermon on "Three Kinds of Good Life."[79] He describes three kinds of conscience by analogy to a church building with the church yard outside where everybody starts, the nave with the pews, where most churchgoers are, and then the chancel or actual sanctuary where a few live.

Churchyard   This is about getting the external rules right—doing good works and doing religious things correctly.

Nave (Pews)   Where they are trying to live faithfully but out of guilt with no joy.

Chancel (altar)For those whose hearts the Spirit has changed and aren't driven by guilt but experience deep joy in their lives in Christ.

Luther describes chancel life this way:

"When the Spirit comes, he makes a pure, free, cheerful, glad, and loving heart—a conscience made righteous by grace, seeking no reward, fearing no punishment, doing everything with joy."

John: So Luther talks about consciences. How does that compare to what we are talking about?

Dave: I think that what old-timers talked about, as being led by your conscience, is what we are calling "being led by the Spirit."

Closer to Christ

Dave: I have been framing the issue as growth in the Christ's Spirit. We can also approach growth by focusing on the other side of God's presence with us, the Christ side of the coin. Perhaps it's easier to envision growth as movement toward becoming more like Christ.

Paul wrote to the Romans that God chose them to be conformed to the likeness of Christ.[80] He wished to be with the Galatians since Christ was in them.[81] He encouraged the Philippians to have the same attitude that Christ did when he humbled himself to become a human.[82] His challenge to the Ephesian congregation was that they should work together to build up the body of Christ, reaching to the very heights of fullness of Christ.[83]

You may find the following insights to be helpful. They are from a research project reported as *Move: What 1,000 Churches Reveal about Spiritual Growth* by Greg Hawkins and Cally Parkinson. They identified growth as a believer's movement through four stages: exploring Christ, growing in Christ, being close to Christ, and being Christ centered. Their lead question was what brings movement to becoming closer to Christ.

The two advanced groups had these core beliefs and attitudes:

- Belief that God is actively involved in my life
- Desire for Jesus to be first in my life
- Willingness to give away my life for Christ
- Existing to know, love, and serve God

Among most common spiritual growth practices for those in the advanced stages were the following:

- Reading and reflecting on the scriptures
- Praying to confess sins and seek guidance
- Tithing

Their top spiritual activities were the following:

- Evangelizing
- Serving those in need
- Having spiritual friendships

Here are some major results:

1. Even the most devoted Christians fall far short of living fully Christ-centered lives.
2. Spiritually stalled or dissatisfied people account for one out of four church congregants.

3. Nothing has a greater impact on spiritual growth than reflection on the scriptures.
4. Church activities don't predict or drive long-term spiritual growth.
5. There is no "killer app" for spiritual growth.
6. Leadership matters.[84]

The first finding shouldn't be surprising. Most devoted Christians fall far short of Christlikeness in their daily living. Because of sin, it is humanly impossible for us to come close to living fully Christ-centered lives. If this is the featured challenge, most who try will fall back on their own human efforts. Thus growth in likeness to Christ comes across as something we could do if we found only the right practices or had enough commitment. Depending on ourselves to grow in Christ is a sure formula for frustration and discouragement. This approach also tends to produce many Christians who don't convey much joy in their lives with Christ.

This emphasis on Christlikeness is also bound to produce spiritually stalled or dissatisfied Christians, the second finding. Why bother trying to do something that seems so discouraging? The research showed that among these one thousand congregations, about one-quarter of members said they are stuck in their movement, their growth. My guess is that the figure for mainline churches would be more like one-half to two-thirds. Guilt from failure to meet a high standard isn't much of a motivator for most Christians. Better is the motivation produced by changes the Spirit works in their hearts. How that happens returns us to the basic issue.

The third finding is key. Spiritual growth happens among Christians who reflect on the scriptures. There are many ways to stay in contact with God's scriptural message of the Father's love, the Son's healing, and the

Spirit's fellowship. Basic is continual exposure, preferably weekly, to explanations and applications of God's word through biblical preaching and teaching. Some do well at setting a specific time for daily devotions and prayer. Others get frustrated. Some find reading difficult and prefer discussion. "Others can spend hours in studying biblical topics on their own." *Amen*

The fourth finding was surprising to the researchers: church activities don't predict or drive long-term spiritual growth. An explanation, of course, can be found in determining what those activities consist of. Do they engage participants in spiritual discussions? One main discovery for me personally in twenty-five years of Lutheran pastoral ministry is how many days and activities go by with just superficial social interactions, even on Sunday mornings, with almost no reaction to the sermon or service. Part of the explanation is that in recent generations mainline churches have drifted in the direction of social organizations like so many others. Most mainline churches have low expectations for changed hearts leading to changed behavior.

The fifth finding underscores the assumption behind my present effort: There is no "killer app" for spiritual growth. Yet leadership matters. That is the sixth finding. Leadership, especially by the pastor, can accomplish two basics: (1) make the destination clear and (2) model the process of growth in the Spirit. Leadership issues will be addressed in the last two discussions.

In most traditional churches, the destination for spiritual growth is neither clear nor even highlighted. Any desired growth seems to be intellectual. What growth in the Spirit involves is properly classified as sanctification that comes after justification. In their search for certainty of salvation, theologians and preachers in my heritage tended to avoid issues of sanctification, the changed life,

David S. Luecke

for fear of it becoming confused with justification, which is God's declaration of eternal salvation by grace without works. But what I am featuring is really an extension of God's grace also to giving freely the gifts the Spirit wants to bring to all believers. We need to be cautious about holding up Christlike living as the goal because it too easily puts the burden back on what we do, not what God does. The goal isn't to become a better Christian in terms of more Christlike behavior. Rather it is to become a more joyful, confident Christian in terms of a changed heart, from which also flows more of the intention and energy to serve others as best as we can.

Ed: I am beginning to see the value of getting the right label. I asked last time why it is important to recognize the Spirit's work behind what we are doing in our church life anyhow.

Dave: Yes, the right label is important. Rather than focusing on what we do, we can see growth as something the Spirit does through us. We too easily miss that the Spirit empowers us to move closer to Christ and then see only the discouraging demands for what we have to do on our own.

Amy: I do want to become a better Christian. What you are doing is challenging us to determine what being a better Christian consists of and how it happens. I would like to do that and look forward to the rest of the spiritual growth process.

Dave: Let me pull together the two strands of Christ and his Spirit in our lives today. Key to understanding Paul is a passage almost completely overlooked in my experience of theology and the preached word. It is in Paul's second letter to the Corinthians, chapter 3. He started commending them for being "a letter from Christ, the results of our ministry, written not with ink but with the Spirit of the living God, not on tablets or stone but on tablets of human hearts." Clearly, Paul was focused on hearts.

In the last verse Paul proclaimed that "we are being transformed into his likeness with ever-increasing glory, which comes from the Lord, who is the Spirit."[85] I take this to mean that the Spirit transforms us into Christlikeness with every increasing glory to God. Such change toward Christlikeness isn't something we can do on our own. His Spirit does it within us. This transformation is progressive over a lifetime; it comes with God's glory ever increasing through us as we grow in the Spirit. The glory isn't our Christlike behavior. It is the heartfelt, joyful use of his gifts to become more fully the person God created each of us to be. Such transformation can happen only through the Spirit's work in our lives. *His workmanship Eph. 2:10*

Questions for Discussion

1. What are your thoughts about a spiritual journey? Has anyone shared his or her personal spiritual journey with you? *It's my Life + purpose   Gal. 2:20*
2. What about "spiritual formation"? Have you heard the term? If so, what does it mean to you? *Phil 3:10*
3. Have there been times when you were especially close to God? What was special? *"Him"*
4. What is your thought about the percentage of people in this congregation who are "stalled" or not growing closer to Christ? *1st Cor. 4:5* ?
5. Why do you think church activities don't predict long-term spiritual growth?

Proverbs 9:10

II Tim. 3:16-17 Amen

It's Focus is human agenda + Jargon. Human achievement Not Spirit work at. God the center

Discussion 8

The Six GROWTH Practices

*G*o to God in worship and prayer.

*R*eceive God's word for you.

*O*pt for self-denial.

give *W*itness to your experiences.

*T*rust God in a new venture.

*H*umble yourself before God.

Zacchaeus had heard good things about this wandering rabbi. He wanted to learn more about Jesus, who was passing through Jericho. But Zacchaeus was short and couldn't see through the crowd. So he climbed a sycamore tree. Up there he did see Jesus. But even better Jesus noticed him, called him by name, and invited himself to his house. Jesus announced that salvation had come to Zacchaeus and his household.

Hold that image of Zacchaeus climbing a tree. That was then. Today we can figuratively climb a tree to get in the way of the Spirit, who is the Spirit of the ascended Christ. In addition to calling us his own in Christ, God wants to refresh and strengthen in each of us the gifts of the Spirit, especially his fruit.

Sometimes Christ's Spirit works in totally unexpected ways. But ordinarily the Spirit breaks through with his life-changing gifts to those who put themselves in his way. They do this by staying close to those who share God's word and applying it to themselves. They do this by recognizing their need and asking the Father to send his Spirit.

Let's return to a discussion of those considering a spiritual growth partnership.

Dave: Have I painted a picture of thriving in the Spirit's gifts that makes sense? Would you like more of what the Spirit can bring into your life as a follower of Christ?

Ed: Sure. But I still think there must be some catch.

Rick: You probably want us to follow some rigid discipline. Plenty of people are trying to tell me that to stay healthy I have to do this particular exercise or eat only that particular food. I have learned to ignore such advice because it just doesn't work for me.

Dave: That reminds me of my church's first missions garage sale. We had about twenty-five pieces of exercise equipment people were getting rid of. They didn't use them anymore. The rewards for using that equipment didn't outweigh the time and discomfort involved. Such happens so often to spiritual programs that get abandoned as too hard or inconvenient. The challenge is to make the benefits of growth in the Spirit more obvious and to highlight practices that best fit an individual believer's temperaments and life situation.

Remember, God wants to give his gifts to you, starting with the great gift of salvation by grace through faith. His attitude of grace extends to gifts the Spirit offers those already in the faith. He can and certainly does impart those gifts without our noticing.

My main point is that we can receive more of those gifts for ourselves when we deliberately seek them. Such seeking is sometimes called a "discipline." Better is to call them "practices." Such spiritual practices cover a range of actions and lifestyles Christians have used over the centuries to be drawn closer to God.

In 1978 Quaker professor Richard J. Foster published *Celebration of Discipline: The Path to Spiritual Growth.* This best-selling book rescued the classical spiritual disciplines from their Roman Catholic context and put them back on the agenda of many Protestants. Foster clarified that they aren't just for spiritual giants found in monasteries but for ordinary Christians in the midst of normal daily activities. He explains,

The Disciplines put us where God can work within us and transform us. By themselves the Spiritual Disciplines can do nothing; they can only get us to the place where something can be done. They are God's means of grace. The inner righteousness we seek is not something that is poured on our heads. God has ordained the Disciplines of the spiritual life as the means by which we are placed where He can bless us.[86]

Foster organized twelve disciplines into these three groupings:

The Inward Disciplines	The Outward Disciplines	The Corporate Disciplines
1. Meditation	5. Simplicity	9. Confession
2. Prayer	6. Solitude	10. Worship
3. Fasting	7. Submission	11. Guidance
4. Study	8. Service	12. Celebration

The featured practices in mainline Protestant churches have certainly been corporate Worship and personal inward Prayer. Traditions differ. My heritage has encouraged inward Study, outward Service, and corporate Confession. Among Protestants those that haven't "caught" are inward Fasting, outward Simplicity, Solitude, or deliberate Submission to another.

Diane: The discipline of corporate guidance seems interesting. What is that all about?

Dave: It is the practice of a younger believer meeting by appointment with a more experienced believer to discuss the faith life of the younger, focusing on whatever he or she had in mind that month, like a faith struggle he or she is having or an area where he or she wants to grow. I was a spiritual director every year with a different student. I would be glad to do that with any from this group who would request it.

Let me add one more perspective on the disciplines before going on to the practices I recommend. In 2014 Nathan Foster, son of the Richard Foster who opened up the twelve disciplines for Protestants, wrote his own book, *The Making of an Ordinary Saint*. He described his frustrations with practicing the disciplines. Then he would recall when his dad whispered with excitement, "Nate, can't you see it? The end result of practicing the disciplines is actually *joy!*" The son explained that the idea of becoming spiritually formed made sense, but the joy part was completely lost on him.[87]

How the Practices Work

Using the acronym GROWTH, I invite you to try these six practices for growing in the Spirit: Go to God in worship and prayer, Receive his word for you, Opt for self-denial, give Witness to your experiences, Trust God in a new venture, and Humble yourself before God.

I hope they help bring you joy as you practice them. I challenge you to deliberately do each of the six practices at least once a week. Then find partners or Christian friends to regularly share your experiences. See if you find yourself growing in insights and feelings that the Spirit can generate within you.

Thoughtfully done, each of these activities or practices can trigger a response in the person doing it—an insight, feeling, or reaction. It is this engagement of head and heart in relating to God at a specific time and place that presents an opportunity for the Spirit to exercise his influence. Each such engagement opens the door, however slightly.

The first two practices—Go to God in worship and prayer and Receive his word for you—can be done by rote or habit without much engagement. The invitation in this GROWTH approach is to consciously break rote routines to reflect on personal experiences at least once a week. Ideally, we should reflect on all our exposures to God's presence and work. Such would be a truly thriving spiritual life. But most people aren't so reflective by temperament. The self-discipline would be to notice and remember your reaction to at least one of the Spirit's approaches. Set a weekly deadline, such as every Sunday evening.

The fourth practice is to give Witness to your experiences. Tell someone else about your time of engagement that week. Here is where the partnership for GROWTH in the Spirit comes in. Find several Christian friends who would agree weekly to share their insights and experiences while doing one or more of the suggested practices. Getting physically together for that purpose is difficult in busy lives. But free conference calls can be arranged to talk and share at a time that is convenient to all.

Here is some psychological theory behind this approach to partnerships for GROWTH in the Spirit. Such growth happens best when you know what you're looking for. The process starts with recognizing the Spirit's movement when you experience it. Name your encounters with the Spirit. Otherwise you might miss their significance. Then share such encounters so their meaning becomes even more important to you. If you don't share an experience, it doesn't "stick" as well. Such momentum might help you then seek more encounters. Then you are well on the way to thriving in the Spirit.

The goal is to weekly name and share one Spirit-related experience in each of the six practices. Over time you may find that such God-related reflections become routine. Then you may also notice that you experience a greater abundance of the Spirit's fruit in your life.

What you can do in your own power is to get engaged with God's word, through which the Spirit can work on you. You can practice such engagement wherever his Word is proclaimed, taught, discussed, remembered, or informally shared. To grow in the Spirit, you do well to put yourself in circumstances that stretch or challenge your responses.

One more action is in your power. You can ask the Father to send the Spirit to you in specific ways. Jesus's teaching on prayer included the invitation to ask, seek and knock, in order to receive. What he really means is this specific promise: If earthly fathers know how to give good gifts to their children, "how much more will your Father in heaven give the Holy Spirit to those who ask him."[88]

Ask for the Spirit to come in specific ways. When you know what you are looking for, you will recognize the Spirit more readily.

Each of the Six Practices

Go to God in Worship and Prayer

Dave: Go to God and Receive his word are basic practices. They are the primary means through which the Spirit acts. From the human perspective, think of these practices as "leaning into God."

Worship and prayer are the same activity of exercising your relationship with God. Worship, including public prayer, is done with other believers. Personal prayer is done privately.

Public worship of Christians over the centuries has revolved around two opposite emphases. One is to bow down before the God far above, the wholly other. This is the God who transcends everything human and earthly. To worship is to show our respect and give reverence.

The other emphasis is on God close to us, whom we encounter in daily life. This is the God who humbled himself and became human in Jesus Christ. Ascended, Christ is with us now through his Spirit. Christ's Spirit is close by us every day; he is immanent within our consciousness. To worship is to open ourselves to the Spirit's work.

The Spirit can do his work in any context where Christians gather around God's word. But for purposes of expecting and recognizing encounters with the Spirit, a more informal setting seems better for making connections with everyday life. From what we can tell about worship in Paul's churches, their sessions were quite informal and left room for unplanned remarks of participants.

My own view is that participants can better open themselves to engagement with the Spirit in a setting that isn't highly scripted and predictable. Churches can organize their worship and organizational routines so tightly that there is little room for the Spirit to bring fresh insights and reactions. Not much change is going to happen among the same people who are always doing the same old things the same old ways.

Rick: Let's get to the prayer part of "go to God." I want to hear more about disciplined prayer every day.

Dave: Spontaneity is important in prayer, too. Consider contrasting a disciplined prayer routine with spontaneous prayer. Some people, but not all, have their time of prayer first thing in the morning in a certain place or posture. Some, but not all, go through a prayer routine, in some cases reciting a prayer by rote. Many do spontaneous prayer, talking with God as circumstances arise, such as facing a problem or following out a train of thought.

The best prayer is really talking with God about something that is on your heart and is thus important to you, whether this conversation emerges in a morning routine or happens spontaneously during the day. Christians have different personalities or temperaments. The basic thought is that who you are is how you pray. I would encourage you later to find out more about your spiritual temperament in our next Discussion.

More helpful for this discussion will be to contrast personal prayer as either a duty or an opportunity. Here is a quote on duty to pray from an old German theologian in my heritage: "Where there is a willingness to pray it is necessary that the time devoted to that purpose be carefully regulated and the regulations strictly adhered to. If prayer is left to inner impulse and fancy, it will practically end in omission, as a result of the slothfulness and luke-warmness of our nature."[89]

That man doesn't have a clue about how the Holy Spirit works and probably doubts the Spirit is aggressively active today.

Here is an alternate view of prayer as an opportunity. This better understanding keys off that Revelation 3 image of Jesus knocking at the door. When we are "in Christ" his Spirit, the Holy Spirit, may several times a day knock on the door of a believer's heart, wanting to initiate a discussion.

The believer who opens the door will enter into meaningful prayer over what is on his or her heart at that moment. God initiates the good things in spiritual life, not us.

Consider another distinction—between long prayers or short ones. A common impression is that the longer the prayer time, the better the prayer. Some giants in spirituality say the opposite. Augustine of Hippo preferred "very brief, quickly dispatched prayers." Thomas Aquinas observed that frequency, not length, is the important issue in prayer; frequent, short prayers are of more worth than fewer, lengthy prayers. Martin Luther preferred "brief prayers pregnant with spirit. The fewer the words the better the prayer." Seventeenth-century mystic Jacob Boehme gave this advice: "Many words are not needed, but only a believing repentant soul." Nineteenth-century Dwight Moody saw the need for constant prayer in the privacy of one's heart. "A man who prays much in private will make short prayers in public." He regarded lengthy public prayers as something akin to religious pretension.

Contemporary Donald G. Bloesch, from whom these quotes came, concludes, "What characterized the great saints was not so much involvement in single protracted prayer or the endless repetition of prayer formulas as the practice of constantly waiting on the Lord, of praying inwardly even when outwardly occupied in daily tasks."[90]

Amber: I have a hard time finding consistency in my prayer life. Are you saying that's okay?

Dave: The answer depends on whether you experience spontaneous discussions with God as your day goes along. If not, then do find a routine that works for you. It might involve saying a memorized prayer. That isn't prayer at its best, but something good might come out of it.

* * *

Here are some questions for reflection and sharing later:

In your worship, when did you last experience a sense of awe in the presence of God, who is wholly beyond anything human? Or a closeness to God as a friend? What triggers these feeling for you?

How and when do you engage in personal prayer? What recently moved you in your prayers?

Receive God's Word for You

There can be considerable overlap between going to God in worship and receiving God's word personally. The point of this second discipline is to take responsibility to explore God's word for fresh applications to your life.

There are many ways to be exposed to the biblical truths. Most directly, of course, is to read the Bible. But some people don't read easily. They receive insights better when they hear it presented and discussed by others. Meditation means thinking about or chewing over the meaning of a specific text at one specific time or over the course of a day.

The Bible is a fascinating collection of inspired writings about God's history with his people. It is the history of salvation truths. There is plenty of head knowledge to be gained through studying it—knowledge about emphases of the individual writers and expectations they had in the context of cultures that were very different from our own. The opportunity to dig deeply is one of the joys of being a pastor.

But reading for personal application brings a different emphasis, especially when the goal is to grow in the Spirit's gifts. However you get engaged in thoughts stimulated by the word, look for the Spirit who wants to bring you comfort for whatever worries you. But also look for the Spirit as he advocates God's will in your life. Be open to thinking about stretching yourself with new and better ways to express God's love and to extend your efforts to bring the healing of grace to others.

What you are looking for in getting engaged with God's message are applications to your life that week. The Spirit works on our motivations. More important than the behavior is the motivation. Spirit-shaped motivation will find ways to express itself—ways that best fit the individual believer in his or her particular situation.

The proposed discipline in this practice of receiving God's word for you is to once a week consciously recognize and remember an application to your life—whether it be a word of comfort or challenge. To grow in the Spirit, lean toward challenges.

* * *

Here are some questions for reflection and sharing later:

When did you last engage with God's word? Hearing a sermon? Reading the Bible?

What is your normal plan for receiving God's word?

What was the topic of the sermon you remember the best?

What part of the Bible would you like to study in greater depth?

Opt for Self Denial

Opt for self denial and Trust God in a new venture are stretch practices. They are meant to move you out of your comfort zone to experience new growth.

The *O* of GROWTH needs explanation. Intuitively "obey" would seem more appropriate, but that raises the question of what needs to be obeyed. In a grace-oriented church, the motivation for certain behaviors is more important than controlling those behaviors. Giving orders is a poor way to induce desired voluntary conduct. Guilt doesn't work well in churches anymore.

What's more practical and effective is to focus on rising

to challenges—especially those Jesus and Paul presented. Jesus told the rich young man to sell all his possessions and then follow him.[91] He told the disciples that anyone who would follow him must deny himself or herself and take up his or her cross daily. Those weren't commands; they were challenges. The rich young man wouldn't even consider giving up anything he owned; he went back to his old way of living. It is the willingness to consider the challenge that is most important. The disciples continually struggled with what they wanted to hang on to from their life before Jesus.

We, too, struggle with how to rise to the countcrintuitive challenge of losing your life so you may save it rather than trying to save your life and losing it.[92] Understand self-denial to mean not insisting on receiving what is rightfully yours in a relationship but to voluntarily giving up something important to you at that moment. Such an act of self-denial, or of losing something from your life, can be a powerful reminder of what you gain as a follower of Christ, thus saving your life by losing it.

Paul didn't give commands to his fellow workers and his churches. He pointed out where they should head in specific situations and told them to figure out how to get there. He told the Ephesians to "submit to one another out of reverence for Christ." Realize who you are in Christ and act accordingly. Recognize that as a challenge. Such submission can be especially difficult between husband and wife.

I am not advocating self-denial and constant submission as a lifestyle. Such might emerge later. But consciously try an act of self-denial or intentional submission once a week. Notice how you feel about it. Deriving benefit from such acts involves being open to the Spirit's influence. See what happens.

Thus, I have chosen "opt" for self denial as the key verb for this act of growth in the Spirit. Such an act of self-denial is in your power. Doing it may involve overcoming a basic fear that something bad will happen to you. Face it as a challenge to your trust in God.

* * *

Here are some questions for later reflection and sharing:

In what relationship did you recently deny yourself for the greater good? How did it feel?

Paul urged "to submit to one another." To whom do you regularly submit?   How does it feel?

What do you think of Jesus's challenge that "whoever will lose his life for me will save it"?

Give *W*itness to Your Experiences

Of the six GROWTH practices, this one assumes you've had some memorable experiences with the Spirit. Tell others what it felt like. These practices are based on biblical truths, as developed in previous discussions. For traditional churches, there is newness in rediscovering Paul's emphasis on the Spirit and his gifts. But the most important newness would be the "nowness" of God's interaction in our lives through the Spirit.

Three psychological principles stand behind this practice of giving witness to your Spirit experiences. To name something is to recognize it as important and make it more memorable. To share makes the experience even more important and memorable. Such sharing encourages others to be on the lookout for the work of the Spirit in their lives. Stories of personal experiences communicate better than the proclaiming of abstract truths.

Practice such witnessing with fellow believers you know and are comfortable with. When you become more confident of your Spirit encounters, move on to sharing some of them with others who aren't churched or aren't even believers. Usually they aren't interested in having the Bible quoted to them. Most no longer see it as a special source of authority. But they may be interested in listening to you if they sense you care about them, and they see something special about the way you live. Your life becomes the basic witness.

In a new members class once, we went around the table with each person introducing himself or herself and answering the question I posed: what brings you here to our church? A young man named a church member who worked in the same facility that he did. His simple explanation was, "I want to be like him." Is there any better witness than that?

* * *

Questions for later reflecting and sharing:

With whom have you recently shared something you experienced in worship or prayer time?

What is the most important part of your Christian life you would want to share with a friend?

Is there someone you admire for his or her Christian walk? Have you shared your appreciation?

Trust God in a New Venture

T is for the verb *trust.* I could have used *faith,* but that brings confusion between the noun for beliefs and the act of having faith in God. Purposely test your trust in God by taking risks on a kingdom adventure. A kingdom adventure is what happens when you take seriously the petition of the Lord's Prayer that "Thy kingdom come." What you are really praying is, "Let it come through me in what I do today. Let me be part of helping God's love work and Christ's grace heal."

Let's consider a kingdom adventure as anything that takes you out of your comfort zone in serving others or in venturing in a new project to express God's love for others. It is a stretch practice.

A new venture can be as small as extending God's love by greeting a stranger, encouraging a store clerk, or stopping to see whether someone is in trouble. It can be a venture of confronting someone who hassling or belittling another. It can be taking on the adventure of a service project on your own or with others at church, or going on a mission trip away from home. It can be committing yourself to a growth partnership like this. Whatever the new venture is has to make sense in your particular situation. Such a venture can be most productive spiritually when taking the initiative involves your fear of losing something.

The classic adventure for trust is to increase your offering to the Lord from off the top of your income.

A really big professional kingdom adventure for me was to take the risk of planting a church from scratch. That is when I discovered a depth of prayer I never experienced before, leading to the curiosity of how ordinary Christians pray and making a research project out of that.

Planting a church is the case Southern Baptist Henry Blackaby used to illustrate his experience of God and to provide a template for others. His thirteen-week Bible study on *Experiencing God* turned into a book that sold eight million copies and was translated into forty-three languages. He advocates seven truths: God is at work in you; he pursues a love relationship with you; he invites you to join him; and he speaks to you. These truths affirm what I'm trying to communicate.

They lead to the fifth experience of a crisis of faith, when you realize you cannot do on your own what God is asking, and if God doesn't help you, you will fail. Then comes a decision whether to believe God for what he wants to do through you. The sixth truth is ultimate surrender to God so his will, not mine, will be done. The seventh is that God will never give you an assignment he won't enable you to complete. "That is what a spiritual gift is—a supernatural empowering to accomplish the assignment God gives you."[93]

I'm not here advocating that you take on a major life-changing kingdom adventure, although that might occur later. Start small. What kind of sharing God's love and grace would take you out of your comfort zone? The discipline in this spiritual practice would be to at least think about such an adventure each week.

* * *

Thoughts for later reflecting and sharing:
Smile and give a friendly greeting to a store clerk or a stranger.
Step up to help someone in need—in a store, in a parking lot, or a neighbor.
Organize or help in a project to serve children or families in need.
Increase your generosity with offerings or possessions.

*H*umble Yourself before God

While humbling logically belongs first, in actuality the practices for spiritual growth can happen in any order. You can jump in anywhere in the six GROWTH practices.

Such humbling is usually called "repentance." In traditional worship the service begins with an act of confession of sins by all and the pronouncement of absolution by the pastor. In the words of the Lord's Prayer, repentance is essentially the realization afresh "Our Father who is in heaven, Hallowed by your name": He is above in heaven, and I am here below him; he is holy, and I am a sinner. Now with that relationship reestablished, get on with talking to God about what's on your mind. Another way of clarifying the relationship is that God can't do much with you when you're full of yourself.

The proposed discipline for this practice is to at least once a week call to mind a moment when you appreciate God's mercy for things you wish you hadn't done. Or recognize when you were thankful for God's grace in giving you what you didn't deserve. Share a mercy or grace moment with someone.

About Sharing Spirit Experiences with Others

Dave: Now, let's get to the question of how to find someone with whom you can share your experiences of the Spirit on a regular basis. Wouldn't it be great if an entire congregation was aware of the practices for GROWTH in the Spirit? Imagine members routinely sharing their Spirit-shaped insights and experiences, offering encouragement to each other.

Amy: Is that possible? When I am with friends at church, we mostly talk about our families and activities.

Dave: In my experience such small talk is mostly what you hear in traditional congregations when participants interact. What excites me is the hope that participants with a greater consciousness of Spirit experiences will find their small talk turning into God talk. Such congregations will enliven and, I think, make a church fellowship more attractive to others. It would convey a greater sense of excitement.

How do we get there? Step by step. I am thankful that you as a group accepted my invitation to come together and discuss what I have presented. I hope you all view anybody else in this group as a partner for sharing your spiritual discoveries and experiences.

Discussion 10 presents how to organize partnerships for Spirit awareness.

Discussion Questions

1. Have you ever heard of "spiritual disciplines"? What do you think they involve, and how do you react to the thought of trying a spiritual discipline?
2. When you think about needed to "go to God" in prayer and worship, what have been the most enjoyable prayer or worship moments for you?
3. What is your preferred way to "receive God's Word"— reading it, hearing it, remembering it, or having it shared by someone else?
4. How easy or hard is it for you to "own the challenge" of denying yourself or submitting to another?
5. Has anyone ever given witness to a spiritual experience? What did you think of this sharing?

6. Have you ever undertaken a "kingdom adventure"—going beyond your comfort zone to serve someone else or trying a new project?
7. When is the last time you humbled yourself before God?

Discussion 9

Discovering Personal Pathways for Encountering the Spirit

For this discussion I'm going to put on my psychologist hat. Psychology today gives us a concept that can help explain how growth in grace can come more naturally.

Temperaments are aspects of an individual's personality that seem innate rather than learned. Such temperaments help determine how we respond to the Spirit's initiatives. The general idea is that who we are is how we pray. *Who We Are Is How We Pray*[94] is the title of the book that opened up this perspective less than thirty years ago. This approach focuses on matching personality and spirituality.

Part of what makes Paul such a great spiritual leader and teacher is that he recognized how the Spirit works in many different ways. His teaching on spiritual gifts in 1 Corinthians 12 is a celebration of diversity. He drove the point home with his analogy of the body of Christ as a human body with so many different parts that have to work together, such as a foot, hand, eye, and ear. Each wants to think it is more important than the other, but all need to work together and honor each other.

Let's return to the discussion of participants willing to become partners in GROWTH of the Spirit.

Dave: That the Christian church paid little attention to spiritual gifts over the centuries helps explain how traditional churches featured only a narrow range of practices to cultivate the presence of God—practices that fit the leaders' preferences.

Rick: Do you think you may again be too hard on traditional churches? I mean, what they did was based on a lot of experience.

Dave: Perhaps I am. What I mean to say is that the traditions appeal mostly to heads and feature rational teaching, with the assumption that hearts will follow. Obviously the Spirit used their work well. But those centuries of tradition assume religious commitment among people who had few alternatives. Such loyalty is quickly disappearing. Now what we see is an insistence on heartfelt experiences. The best way to connect with others is to give more attention to their temperaments and feelings by becoming more aware of your own temperament and feelings as the Spirit works to transform you.

As mentioned earlier, the book that opened up this new approach is *Who We Are Is How We Pray* by Charles Keating in 1987. It is now in its ninth printing. He applied categories from the very popular Myers-Briggs Personality Inventory, which is administered two million times a year in corporations. This Inventory yields sixteen combinations of personality traits distinguished by letters such as ESFP or INTJ. I have worked it through but concluded from experience that it is too complicated to teach easily, and it is hard to move to applications for prayer and worship.

Much easier to understand is David Kolb's Learning Style Inventory, which describes different ways we learn and deal with ideas. Some people easily handle abstract ideas; others cannot get past concrete meanings. Some learn by observation, others by testing for what works.

All I want to say here is that these distinctions help to explain why communication is so hard in a congregation. Preachers deal in abstractions like doctrines, while most hearers have to be given concrete examples, best done with stories. Some develop their own ideas from observations, while others look for someone else's plan that they apply. Most businesspeople are oriented to concrete application. Philosophers, economists, and theologians like to conceptualize things abstractly. Many pastors tend to think like engineers, who apply someone else's abstract theory. But more are like businesspeople who want to apply a specific plan someone else engineered.

The simplest way to illustrate what is involved is Gary Thomas's very readable *Sacred Pathways: Discover Your Soul's Pathway to God.*[95] He identifies nine temperaments and the pathway that can best draw each closer to God. Thomas doesn't identify the theory he applies here. He says he was led to these pathways based on biblical personalities, historic church movements, and various personality temperaments. He is clearly a creative church theorist who knows how to make practical applications. His book has the inventories for you so you can discover your preferred pathways.

Thomas narrows the options to nine that intuitively make sense and can be found in the scriptures. I am going to add a tenth. These are the following:

- The Naturalist: Loving God Out-of-Doors. Finds a walk through the woods to be very conducive to prayer.
- The Sensate: Loving God with the Senses. Wants to be lost in awe, beauty, and splendor of God.
- The Traditionalist: Loving God through Ritual and Symbol. Likes structured worship with symbols and sacraments.
- The Ascetic: Loving God in Solitude and Simplicity. Wants to be left alone in prayer.
- The Activist: Loving God through Confrontation. Serves a God of justice, and church fills a need to recharge batteries.

- The Caregiver: Loving God by Loving Others. Serves God by serving others.
- The Enthusiast: Loving God with Mystery and Celebration. Wants to be inspired by joyful celebration.
- The Contemplative: Loving God through Contemplation. Likes images of loving Father and Bridegroom.
- The Intellectual: Loving God with the Mind. Drawn to explore basic issues in theology and church life.
- The Developer: Loving God by Bringing Out the Best in Others. Wants to help others use their God-given talents and interests to best serve God and others.

In the movie *Chariots of Fire*, Olympian runner Eric Liddell says that "when I run I feel God's pleasure." The question for you is, in which of these ten temperaments do you best feel God's pleasure?

The challenge is for each pursuer of the Holy Spirit is to find the most productive pathway. For myself, enjoying a naturalist walk in the woods or observing a sunrise doesn't do much. I live in a church body with many traditionalists, but symbols and liturgy don't seem to move me the ways so many others report. I admire enthusiasts, but more from afar, and I tend not to be very emotional. I do enjoy and am enriched by activist adventures of sensing a direction the Spirit is leading and then seeing what emerges. But the intellectual is my basic pathway. I enjoy the Spirit most when I'm trying to figure out how he has worked in the past and is working now. I am also a developer, as I will explain later.

So, just from what little I have said, which pathway seems to work best for you?

Amber: I am one of those who enjoys hiking in the woods and noticing beautiful sunsets. They remind me of the Creator God.

John: I attend the traditional worship service and do think about symbols, like the cross, the vestments the pastor wears, and the body and blood of Christ in the sacrament. When I am in the sanctuary, I feel like I am in the presence of God.

Amy: I like the contemporary service and am often moved by the singing. I appreciate the informality and the sense of freshness. I feel like the Spirit is close at hand.

Dave: What about the caregivers? I appreciate seeing them in action and how it seems to come naturally. It certainly doesn't for me.

Gail: I am thankful for the blessing of my children. When I'm caring for them, I feel like I am doing what God put me on earth to do. I get frustrated with too many demands and not having enough time. But when I step back and get perspective, I feel God is close.

Dave: Getting perspective on what's important is basic to recognizing the Spirit at work and appreciating the grace of God's gifts. Remember, the basic fruit of the Spirit is feelings like love, joy, and peace. In your Christian walk, you want to look for the circumstances where those uplifting feelings seem to come naturally.

I was much impressed when I read about how Ignatius Loyola, founder of the Catholic Jesuit order, established his famous spiritual discipline. He tried different methods and judged their results by examining the feelings they left him with, seeing whether they steadied and increased his desire for closeness to God or left it wanting. Those that brought about an increasing "sweetness," he continued.[96]

John: I have always thought the best way to draw closer to Christ is to read his word. Now you are saying there are many different ways?

Dave: There are many different ways to draw closer to God, but all are variations on how the Spirit can work on you through the good news conveyed in the scriptures.

Ministry as Gardening

Dave: I have been emphasizing that the Spirit grows fruit in a believer's life. This can lead to the analogy of ministry as planting and watering seeds of God's kingdom. Discussion 5 on special motivation by the Spirit led to the analogy of ministry as coaching. Paul's description of the Corinthian congregation as God's field and building suggests other analogies.[97] Let's consider God's field here. Discussion 10 will develop God's building.

When you are looking at your congregation through the eyes of Paul, what kind of field do you see? Farmers are used to looking at a field of only one crop, be it wheat, corn, or soybeans. But given Paul's conviction that a variety of special giftings is present among different people, I think he envisioned a congregation as a garden with many fruit trees, vegetables, and even flowers that blend together into a God-pleasing integrated whole, just like a garden of Eden.

Paul wasn't a one-crop farmer, a one-size-fits-all spiritual leader. He was a very skilled gardener who knew how best to tend to different kinds of plants to bring each to its full fruition. He recognized that some of the people the Spirit brought into the fellowships were specially blessed to teach and preach well, some to care for others, some to contribute generously, and others to administer how these efforts can be brought together for the common good of the fellowship. Paul could recognize something special that a specific individual could bring to his or her shared life, and he could sense how to get that participant into action. By God-implanted instinct, he could see what human resource specialists in management try to do today with elaborate tests and motivation techniques to better guide workers to where they could best contribute to the common good of a corporation.

When Paul laid a foundation for a congregation, he wasn't just teaching them the life-changing truths of what God offers in Jesus Christ through his Spirit. He also modeled how the Spirit works differently in individuals. He showed how the leadership challenge is to build up and integrate growth-stimulating relationships among those who responded to the new gospel of grace he proclaimed. Get the foundation of grace-oriented, Spirit-inspired relationships right, and a lasting and fruitful local body of Christ is easier to build up into a unique fellowship of the Holy Spirit.

In Discussion 10 I am going to promote the image of ministry as building. We'll explore what Paul meant when he described himself as a master builder. Discussion 10 will also group the planter, gardener, coach, and builder together and describe it a "developer's approach to ministry." This stands in contrast to the shepherd image so extensively used in traditional churches.

I propose that this old village-oriented approach of a shepherd has become outmoded by the rapid social changes causing the accelerating withering of traditional churches. Healthy congregations today are doing innovative ministry such as a developer would.

Discussion Questions

1. What do you think of the claim that "who you are is how you pray"?
2. Would you consider yourself to be someone who enjoys thinking about doctrine or someone who needs concrete examples?

3. Look over the ten pathways described earlier in this chapter. Which ones do you think fit you?
4. Do you have experience tending to a garden with many different kinds of plants? What's involved?
5. What do you think about viewing a congregation as a garden with a variety of plants?

Part 4: Leading Spiritual Growth in a Congregation

Discussion 10

Partnering to Build Up the Fellowship of the Holy Spirit

Add "fellowship" to the Spirit's job description. He claims and changes hearts in Christ's name. He grows fruit like love, joy and peace in those hearts. He motivates believers to love and serve others. And he draws them into sharing together their life in Christ.

Paul considered such fellowship-making to be the most distinctive of the Spirit's work within the Triune God. In his benediction to the Corinthians he blessed them with "the *grace* of the Lord Jesus Christ, the *love* of God and the *fellowship* of the Holy Spirit."

In this summary by Paul, the distinctive contribution of the Father is his love and the contribution of the Son is his grace. Watch for the Spirit's fellowship wherever God's love is working and Christ's grace is healing. God the Father's love is constant. When the Son came into this world, he earned our salvation through his death and resurrection, which is now offered by grace as a free gift. Since Christ's ascension, the Spirit extends God's love by bringing individuals into fellowship with God and into the fellowship of Christians with each other.

Our job, then, is to extend the Father's love and promote the healing of Christ's grace. What are we supposed to do with the Spirit's fellowship? Enjoy it, of course, just as we are meant to be strengthened by God's love and encouraged by Jesus's grace. Enriched, then we are called to work together to build up the fellowship. To build up is Paul's special emphasis.

We return to the discussion among those considering whether to become partners for spiritual growth.

Dave: Let me introduce the "fellowship of the Holy Spirit" by telling you about an experience I had with a brand-new Protestant congregation in the Russian city of Tver, about ninety miles northwest of Moscow. I was with a Church Growth teaching team for a conference in that capital city. This was just a few years after the collapse of communism in Russia.

My weekend assignment was to lead a team to preach and teach in this new congregation in Tver. It started when a young woman went to a crusade in Moscow and became a Christian. She went home to share her excitement with her husband. An effective evangelist, she brought together dozens of other into the congregation, for which her husband became pastor. He had been a Christian for only two years. The Sunday I was there had about three hundred in attendance, meeting in a dilapidated Russian movie theater. I was amazed to see how heavily underlined their personal Bibles were. Few had held a Bible more than a year or two.

This was pristine Christian fellowship, similar to the birth of the Christian church on Pentecost in Jerusalem. In Tver the Spirit was obviously at work, drawing trained atheists into a growing relationship with Christ and at the same time prompting them to seek out each other to learn more about what happened to them and to encourage each other in a still-hostile environment.

Imagine if only a third of that energy could be transferred into a traditional Protestant congregation in America. We have to believe the same Spirit at work in Tver is the one who wants to influence and excite believers and churches here and now. They were experiencing newness and nowness. Traditional churches too often stay focused on the old and usually leave the Spirit back in biblical times. They see him now only vaguely in the background.

I would like for us to discuss how your church can become more like the Tver church. This is a task calling for creative leadership in an existing congregation.

"Build Up" the "Fellowship" of the Holy Spirit

Two concepts are key to Paul's understanding of what should be happening in a Christian congregation. One names the object of attention—the "fellowship" of the Spirit. The other names what to do with it—"build up" this unique God-given fellowship. We will need to understand both in Paul's original meaning in order to appreciate the challenge to form a Partnership for Spiritual Growth that I am asking you to join.

"Partnership" is a good translation of the original word for fellowship—*koinonia*, having something in common. The usual English word is "fellowship." "Partnership" is a heavier word that today conveys more seriousness than the now-lightweight "fellowship." Lawyers aspire to be "partners" owning a law firm. To be a partner in a fellowship is to make a serious commitment to others, like spending time together sharing experiences of the Spirit and building each other up.

Out of curiosity, let me ask what comes to mind when you think of fellowship in connection with a church?

Amber: I think of it as something a church does when it gets together to socialize, like getting together after a worship service or having a dinner together. For some reason cookies and coffee come to mind.

Rick: I hear it as an activity—to fellowship with someone. I think it means to socialize and make light conversation with someone.

Dave: That is what I expected—fellowship as a superficial social activity. The biblical concept of "fellowship" has become trivialized. It has lost its original meaning. I have seen "to fellowship" listed as one of the purposes of a congregation— an add-on to their basic efforts to worship, educate, spread the Gospel, serve and also to fellowship.

A better view is that a congregation is a fellowship of the Holy Spirit which exists to help each other worship, grow in the word, spread the gospel and serve others. It is this underlying fellowship of the Spirit which makes a gathering of Christians more than just a social organization.

It helps to go back to the original word for "fellowship"— *koinonia*. The root word means "common," or "to have something in common." The meaning of *koinonia* is to share something with somebody. It is used for participating in Christ's body and blood and sharing this experience with other partakers.[98] Another word for the Lord's Supper is "communion"—having in common. Fellowship with Christ also means living, suffering, dying, and reigning with him. It means being motivated and enriched by the Spirit. You can't get more fundamental than being in fellowship with Christ through his Spirit.

Fellowship also carries the meaning of sharing with others this fellowship with Christ and his Spirit.[99] For Paul, the Spirit was *among* individual believers, drawing them together and making of them a sum greater than the separate parts, such as a human body—indeed they become the body of Christ.[100] Those the Spirit gathers then have the common purpose of inviting the Spirit to guide their personal Christian lives and walk together.

In a previous discussion, I shared my view that mainline churches are in decline partly because they have drifted into thinking and acting like just one of many social organizations with their vocabulary of "joining" and getting "volunteers" "involved." Indeed the distinctive nature of a spiritual fellowship is getting harder to find among mainline churches. Reclaiming the Spirit as an active force today who gives special life to a congregation would be a good start restoring vitality to traditional Protestant congregations.

"Building up" what is already in a congregation is a basic metaphor Paul used extensively—twenty eight times in twenty three different passages. The root *oikos-domeo* literally means "house to assemble." By extension the house becomes the household. Paul extended it to mean the fellowship, a congregation.

He told the Ephesians they were members of God's household, with Christ as the chief cornerstone. "In him the whole building is joined together and rises to become a holy temple in the Lord. And in him you too are being built up together to become a dwelling in which God lives by his Spirit."[101]

For Paul, to build up the fellowship was the fundamental task of ministry. To the Corinthians he described himself as the architect, or the master builder, and they are "God's building."[102] The job of leaders is "to prepare God's people for works of service, so that the body of Christ may be built up to reach the very heights of the fullness of Christ."[103]

Paul used the body of Christ and the fellowship of the Holy Spirit interchangeably. They both describe the fundamental nature of a local congregation. "Building up" goes with the metaphor of a building. "Growing" goes with the alternate metaphor of an organic body. To the Corinthians he explained that God grew the seed Paul planted and Apollos watered.[104]

Paul referred to "the body of Christ" once, in the passage cited above. Twice he used "the fellowship of the Holy Spirit".[105] I think focusing on the Spirit clarifies that this fellowship is something happening right now. We share our common identity in Christ, but that can remain mostly a symbol. It is the Spirit that energizes the sharing we are called to do. The Spirit is waiting for opportunities to breathe new motivation and focus into a congregation.

This goal of building up the fellowship clearly implies avoiding or resolving conflict. Caution is in order lest interpreting personal experiences of the Spirit lead a participant to think or imply that he or she is somehow a better Christian than the others in the fellowship. Even at the beginning in Paul's churches some claimed to have the Spirit while others did not. Paul's answer was the radical notion that every believer has the Spirit, and fellowships should appreciate whatever manifestations of the Spirit appear among its members.

In the 1960s and 70s some traditional churches (especially Episcopalian, Lutheran and Catholic) witnessed the charismatic movement. This was among members who experienced the Spirit's gift of speaking in strange tongues and wanted to share their joy at what the Spirit was doing within them. The movement caused divisiveness in congregations. The many who didn't receive this gift often thought they were being regarded as second-class

Christians. The whole topic of the Spirit's gifts was new to the heritage of traditional churches.

Forty years later we should be able to read the relevant biblical passages more calmly with greater openness to the non-controversial gifts the Spirit wants to give.

Paul encouraged the Corinthians, who were eager to have spiritual gifts, to excel in gifts that build up the church, and speaking in tongues isn't one of those. Knowledge puffs up but love builds up. Everything is permissible but not everything builds up fellowship; seek not your own good but the good of others. To the Romans, make every effort to do what leads to peace and building up the fellowship. He said in several places that if what you're saying or doing doesn't build up the fellowship, then don't do it.[106] May this simple instruction guide all believers in choosing what to say and do in their Spirit-inspired fellowship as well as in all their other relationships.

Partnering to Grow in the Fellowship of the Holy Spirit

I have been using the word "partner" since our first discussion, inviting our group to become partners for spiritual growth. I recruited you as a pilot group. Thank you for the generosity of your time for letting me work out the biblical job description for the Spirit and the implications for our life in Christ now.

But we have only begun to act as partners. The next stage is when you spend time together actually sharing what you experienced in doing the six GROWTH practices. At the end of this session, I want to get you organized into groups of five to seven. Then we can work out arrangements for sharing your experiences in weekly get-togethers. Aim for at least four such sharing sessions.

Even if you grow in the Spirit just a little bit in four weeks, I hope you will find the experience rewarding and will want to continue to share with others your encounters with the Spirit as they occur.

Bill: Remind me. What are those benefits?

Dave: You already have eternal salvation, so that isn't involved. Another word for what I am promoting is that you become more mindful of the Spirit's work in your life. Christ's Spirit is continually trying to get your attention so that he can enter your thoughts and make changes in your inner disposition, your heart. He wants you to find higher meaning and joy in your life. He wants to move you along in your personal journey of growth in living the life God wants for you.

The Spirit's gifts are fresh motivation and energy to serve, as well as growing his fruit in you. Think joy, peace, hope, trust, patience. I can't guarantee that if you become more aware of the Spirit in and around you that you will find more of those qualities in your life. But, humanly speaking, the odds are much better when you consciously expect and pray for the Spirit to draw you closer to God in specific ways.

What would this awareness look like? In one of our earliest discussions I gave you this definition: Recognize Christ's Spirit at work in situations that bring you better understanding of God's ways and that arouse in you special feelings like peace, joy, awe, unity, or fresh energy. We can expect those understandings and feelings when we experience or observe the love of God at work and the grace of Christ bringing freedom into our lives.

To become closer to God may seem like an overwhelming task—one more burden to add to all the others that make daily life a challenge. Indeed it would be—if we expected to accomplish this on our own. But you can walk with the Spirit, who will lead and empower you. He can do that better when you're aware of his initiatives.

I was tremendously excited and encouraged by the Christian fellowship I saw in Tver, Russia. I think Christians in many churches would be happy to see even just some of that fellowship life in their congregation.

Would you be willing to extend your vision of what could happen in this congregation? Think of what the Spirit could do if naming, sharing, and seeking more encounters with the Spirit would become a habit in this congregation.

Sarah: I am still thinking about meeting in four more sessions. Will this bigger effort take more time?

Dave: We are all protective of our time. What I have in mind would involve leadership time and effort by a few people. For the rest, it isn't so much new time as adding focus to how you currently spend your time.

To start, think about inviting others beyond this group to participate in four sessions of Spot-the-Spirit Discussion, each with a presentation on a video followed by a small group discussion experience. These could be done over four Sunday morning study sessions or in already-established evening small group gatherings. Or the four could be done in one four to five hour workshop on a Saturday morning and early afternoon or even on Sunday afternoon.

A 32-page Guide plus DVDs of my introductory presentations for these four sessions can be obtained from www.GROWTHintheSpirit.church.

The larger group would then divide into five to seven-person small groups that agree to meet frequently and talk about the six GROWTH practices. One of the benefits of the communication revolution in the past several decades is that we can get even seven together on a free conference call without leaving home and at a time most convenient to all.

I can envision repeating this process of four sessions of Spot-the-Spirit Discussions two or three times over a fall, winter, and spring. In effect each would be a temporary spiritual growth partnership. The aim for the first year would be to have five percent of the fellowship consider themselves partners in expecting and sharing Spirit encounters. I would ask all those to pray that the Spirit would turn this beginning into an expanding movement.

Imagine what would happen if half of the congregation members became part of a really big partnership to name, share, and seek encounters with the Spirit. This congregation would have a new culture where Spirit awareness and God talk come naturally. Imagine the excitement level!

Two kinds of leaders would be needed. One would be teachers who can oversee the initial four sessions of Spot-the-Spirit Discussions, arranging for the presentations and overseeing the small group discussion experiences. Another is somebody gifted in administration who can arrange occasions for the follow-up sharing experiences. This might be as simple as setting up and initiating those weekly conference calls among the small group participants. Some of these groups might want to organize themselves to continue their conversations. There is no predicting how the Spirit will move among specific believers at specific times.

This Spirit-awareness effort would certainly benefit from spiritual growth planning team of four to five members who would coordinate efforts and dream big.

They can work out solutions to the problems that will inevitably happen. They might find a growing interest among partners to expand their understanding of how the Father, Son, and Holy Spirit work together through focused Bible studies. Certainly the pastor should be aware of what these partners are thinking and doing. Wisdom is needed. This basic spiritual effort will not go far without the spiritual leader's endorsement and support.

In that Tver congregation, those new Christians had heavily underlined Bibles. Usually applying Bible insights leads to a greater experience of the Spirit. For most of those new Christians, however, the experience came first and drove them into the scriptures to learn more. The same increased interest in God's word might happen, too, among believers who become more aware of the Spirit in their midst.

Revitalizing an Existing Congregation

Only God knows where these efforts may go. But if pursued with a commitment to build up the fellowship, the results should be good. Greater Spirit awareness can lead to many new blessings and even renewal. Revitalized by the gifts of the Spirit, a congregation might even turn around its numeric decline.

The only way to revitalize a congregation is to renew the people in it. Lots of congregations have tried to turn around decline with more and new programs and advertising. But the best way to attract new participants is to have members who are excited about their relationship with Christ and eager to talk about what his Spirit is doing in their lives. Only the Spirit can bring that about.

But not much is going to happen if we stay passive. What we can humanly do is learn from Paul how to increase our expectations of the Spirit's work in our midst. This means getting better at recognizing his special gifts that change lives. Jesus himself said that if you want more of the Holy Spirit, ask the Father, who promises to give the Holy Spirit to those who seek him.[107]

Sometimes the Spirit surprises and comes quickly with might. I saw this in the church in Tver. It is happening in other parts of the world today. In traditional mainline churches he did come slowly and consistently over the decades when they were growing. For those of us in those traditional churches, the one clear action we can take now is to prayfully expect and share encounters with the Spirit in our personal and church life.

Observations on Traditional Church Organization and Culture

What made the church in Tver so exciting is that they was still figuring out its formal organization as needs arose, just as the earliest Christians were doing in the first century. These new Tver Christians were quite happy to include and care for anyone who was interested in what they were doing. They were not locked into traditions that had become dysfunctional, as has happened over the centuries with traditional mainline Protestant churches.

1. Traditional churches need to develop better ministry structures

Many existing congregations today have formal organizations defined, for instance, in their constitution. For mainline church bodies such organizational form is called their "polity" as determined at their beginnings 300 to 500 years ago. That word comes from the root giving us "police." The historic emphasis is on preventing bad things from happening, as was appropriate when those church bodies were healthy and could assume loyalty. Now most withering congregations need organized ways to help better initiatives and ministries happen. The committee structure of the last half-century does not work well anymore.

A useful distinction today is between governance structure

and ministry structure. Governance is concerned with making major decisions about a congregation's policies and property. Ministry structure helps give focus and support to doers of services and ministries. Doers typically don't want to have to sit on standing committees required to meet monthly. Let them work out their own arrangements for coordinating what they want to do. Such structure of ministry teams can be separate from the governance structure.

Many withering congregations are finding that they can't recruit enough members to fill all the committee positions called for in their constitution. The typical complaint is, We can't get anybody to do anything. Today, I think, the key mandate for church leadership is, Don't waste anyone's time. In many cases the constitutional organization structure has become dysfunctional. Let it die out. Rather, focus attention on ministry teams, which may well be temporary and frequently take on new forms.

In this discussion I have highlighted and named two ministry teams. One I called Partnership for Spiritual Growth. There can be many such temporary partnerships at work at the same time. The other I called a Spiritual Growth Planning Team. Only one of these, it also can exist outside the governance structure.

Most withering congregations will welcome initiatives that offer hope of new vitality. If the need for control is too strong to permit innovations, such a church is probably in a death spiral. Church bodies would do well to innovate a hospice program for dying congregations, of which there are now thousands in most mainline denominations.

2. **Traditional churches need to provide better supervision of ministry**

Most congregations today provide inadequate supervision for those who feel called and energized by the Spirit to do specific ministries in a fellowship. One of the results of raising Spirit awareness in a congregation is an increase in the number of participants who feel gifted by the Spirit to contribute to the common good. Ways need to be developed to provide them guidance and support. Providing for better supervision applies to paid staff as well, including the pastor.

"Supervision" can be a negative word when thought of in governance terms—being sure you don't do anything wrong. But it becomes a positive when thought of in management terms of providing structure and support to a worker. Providing structure is to clarify goals, to guide efforts and to offer knowledge and technical assistance. Providing support is to create a feeling of approval, to recognize individuality and to provide fair treatment. Actually, providing for structure becomes a basic way of offering support.

The Biblical word for supervisor means overseer. We translate that word as bishop. There is considerable evidence that in Paul's churches the bishop was the lead elder who oversaw the smaller house churches in which thirty or so participants would meet weekly. Today this typically would be the pastor of a large congregation. There is no avoiding the necessity for pastors of such churches to be a good supervisor or manager. If not the preaching or teaching pastor, then someone on the staff has to fulfill this administrative function.

More discussion of these organizational perspectives can be found in Chapter 9 and 10 of my 2010 publication Builder *Ministry in the 21st Century*.[108]

3. Traditional churches need to fine-tune their church culture

Each congregation has its own a distinctive culture within the context of the specialized church culture fostered by each denomination. The changes happening in the broader American social culture today can be seen as a call to fine-tune church cultures. For traditional Protestants that call amounts to raising Spirit awareness and expectations

A culture is an integrated pattern of knowledge, beliefs, and behaviors that determines what is learned and transmitted to future generations. Churches are usually very good at presenting the knowledge and values they stand for. But working these out in distinctive behaviors of the participants is typically a weakness, especially when relying on guilt as the motivator. Shaping distinctive Christian behaviors becomes a special challenge in grace-oriented churches that emphasize how we are saved by God's free gift, not by the good behaviors we do. As I have argued, the key to changed behaviors is expecting and fostering the work of Christ's Spirit especially in the form of the fruit he produces.

"How to Shape a More Spirit-oriented Church Culture" is part 4 of my 2014 publication *Your Encounters with the Holy Spirit*.[109] In a church three key steps are to Preach the motivation, Model the behaviors and Organize opportunities.

Changing corporate cultures is a huge topic in business schools these days. Few businesses as well as social and educational institutions have escaped the pressure brought by more competition and higher expectations for what is provided. The same pressures now exist for traditional church institutions—Protestant as well as Roman Catholic.

Here are a few basics for fine-tuning a culture:

- Such change is anxiety-provoking and inevitably brings conflict.
- Strong leadership is needed to put change into effect.
- Leaders have to earn the right to be followed in new behaviors.
- A more effective culture arises through shared experiences of success.
- Culture trumps vision.

Previous discussions have highlighted metaphors Paul used to describe his work as a church leader: building up, planting, gardening and coaching. These open up new perspectives on congregational ministry today that are different from the old analogy of shepherding members of a congregation. I develop them in the following Eleventh Discussion of the Developer Model for Spirit-Based Ministry.

Discussion Questions

1. Have you ever seen or experienced a Christian congregation overflowing with energy, like the one in Tver Russia?
2. Would you like to see more "Spirit mindfulness" in your congregation?
3. IIow interested would you bc in committing to and experiencing a small partnership for spiritual growth?
4. Would you consider partnering with additional others in your church to build up the fellowship of the Holy Spirit?
5. How open are you to fine-tuning your church's culture?

Discussion 11

The Developer Model for Spirit-Based Ministry

The previous discussions pointed to appropriate metaphors for ministries that best support the work of Christ's Spirit: planter, gardener, coach, and builder. Put them together, and you have what a developer does: he or she brings about something more or better in the future than what exists now. Call this the developer model of ministry.

The developer model stands in contrast to the shepherd model that was dominant in the heritage of mainline church bodies since the Reformation. From the beginning into the twentieth century, seven out of eight congregations were in villages or small towns organized into parishes, a geographic term. The pastor, parson, or vicar was state supported and supervised. The parishioners really had little to say about their church life. They were like sheep in need of a shepherd to feed and protect them. This metaphor, still beloved by some today, was believable then because most were barely literate. The term *clerical* for the clergy pastor carries with it the basic function of writing and handling words, like clerical staff do today in an office. Back then the pastor was often the only one who could do this.

In the twentieth century, several movements happened. One is the major migration from the country to the city, and with that came the loss of a strong sense of parish or even community. The other is the rise of public education, whereby first almost all had a grade school education and now almost all a high school education. About one-quarter of the national population is college educated, and many of those have graduate degrees. They aren't used to thinking of themselves as helpless sheep. Nor do many still carry with them a sense of loyalty to the church body of their parents.

Mainline church bodies have another hangover from the village setting that shaped their ministry practices. Villages present strong pressure for conformity. Most villagers would resist a few becoming very different from the rest. At least that is my explanation for why mainline churches have such little emphasis on personal spiritual growth and so few resources beyond increasing knowledge. There would be strong resistance by the others to be somehow considered lower-class Christians. Today most urban and suburban congregations have a minimal sense of community and thus are open to participants choosing personal expressions that are different from their own.

Basic to a development model of congregational leadership is changing what exists now. The planter sets each seed in the ground in anticipation that it will bring a yield of thirty or one hundred times. The gardener cultivates the soil so each type of plant will get just the right water, fertilizer, and weeding to grow to its maximum. The coach assesses the motivation of each player and tries to arrange opportunities for that player to reach maximum performance and accomplishment. The builder focuses on relationships and strives to build up as many God-pleasing relationships as possible; each set a temple in which God lives by his Spirit.

The inherited shepherd model of leadership, in contrast, aims to maintain what exists. The church is there to minister to members going through their stages of life from birth to death. They change, but the church doesn't; it is intended to be an anchor of stability. The only welcome change might be construction of a new church facility.

The church shepherd today marches on, doing the same things the same way with the same people, hoping something will happen to turn around decline and perhaps secretly hoping these members will support his salary and benefits until retirement.

The church planter/gardener/coach/builder would face the same congregation and communicate that "something in what we are doing here has to change. We have to plant more seeds of the kingdom; we have to cultivate the soil differently." Such a pastor would focus on building up new relationships within the congregation and the community, and on coaching members who have the potential for doing more ministry and leadership.

Both the shepherd model and developer model focus on the congregation, the basic unit of church where Christian faith, life, and witness are worked out. The main goal of the shepherd model is to feed and protect participants. It focuses on individuals, comforting them in their times of difficulty; their personal spiritual growth in practice isn't a high priority. The goal of the developer model is to awaken new insights and challenge participants to higher levels of spiritual growth. This is typically done by building up relationships among similarly minded participants.

Each model has its own understanding of how to apply God's word, what the basic tasks are, and what should be emphasized. Driving each model are differing concepts of what ministry is and who does it.

How Shepherds See Their Job

To appreciate the shepherd model of ministry at its best, think of a village in England or Saxony in the early nineteenth century or a small town in Iowa in the early twentieth century. The people are tied to the land through their farms; they expect to be there for life. Everybody knows almost everybody else; they shop together, send their children to the same school, and solve community problems together. They know each other's foibles and are quite conscious of what others think of them. The sense of community is strong and includes pressures to be like everyone else.

In the shepherd model the basic ministry task is to guide the flock gathered in that area, the members in the geographic parish, through their personal lives. Their church gives them identity, and their loyalty is expected. The minister feeds and protects. This is done by surrounding them repeatedly and as much as possible with God's truth conveyed through sermons, lessons, worship forms, and visible symbols as well as baptisms, weddings, and funerals. The intent is to extend and deepen a participant's understanding of life with God in all its richness. This becomes a matter of reminding them of who they are. The care of souls offers the comfort of God's love in crises.

The shepherd model emphasizes the proclamation of God's word. This is the primary responsibility of the pastor. The relevance and importance of God's word in the inspired words of scripture are a given; the need is to make fresh application. Preaching is based on the lectionary, the assigned readings for the week. The sacraments can be powerful sources of comfort for those who rightly understand them, and considerable time is devoted to teaching and celebrating them. Formalized liturgical worship best conveys the richness of God's truth and presence, and repetition is good. Formal, written prayers are highly valued, and participants are encouraged to do any other prayer in the privacy of their own personal prayer lives.

Because correct biblical knowledge is so important for feeding and protecting the fellowship, the shepherd needs to have special seminary training leading to formal ordination, and any others doing ministry need similar preparation. Conventionally this pastor does all the important word ministries of preaching, teaching, leading worship, and offering pastoral care. All others help with secondary support work. The shepherd model features a two-part distinction within churches: the clergy and everyone else, the laity.

How Developers See Their Job

The ministry of the developer, on the other hand, aims to expand and build up people's connections with Christ and with each other. Ministry is all about relationships. Supplemental to God's truth as a symbol, like doctrine, is God's truth as an encounter and experience. The appeal is as much to hearts as it is to heads. Awakening and encouraging new experiences are tasks added to feeding and protecting. Challenge is in a steady rhythm with comfort.

The development model revolves around making new connections within the congregation and in the community. All members, as the priesthood of believers, are seen as the ministers, adding their service to that of others and multiplying God-focused relationships. Informal prayer shared among participants helps build relationships.

The word of God is to be communicated, not just proclaimed. Keeping the attention of the hearers and addressing their perceived needs are high priorities. This often means topical preaching using a variety of communication techniques. The sacraments are valued but no more than the well-communicated word. Developers are more inclined to experiment with new forms of worship, looking for what engages the participants. This usually means an informal style with moments of spontaneity. The singing is usually led by a worship team, and the songs are contemporary, written in the past decade or so. The organ is replaced with drums and guitars. Many congregations offer both a continuation of traditional worship and also what is now popularly called "contemporary worship."

Contrasting Perspectives on Church Culture

The different approaches to worship amount to contrasting perspectives on church culture. The shepherd model characteristically depends on a distinctive traditional church culture that separates church life from everyday life, language, and music. Within this culture is safety. This assumption often leads to an emphasis on keeping up appearances in a way that doesn't encourage participants to share their struggles. This small-town heritage assumes community already exists among participants. Aside from special "fellowship" events, little attention is given to community building.

The developer model, in contrast, is more open to the social community around the church, including those whose lifestyles and challenges can often be very different from those of traditional church people. Church planters/gardeners/coaches/builders are usually more willing to meet people where they are with their language and music. Much effort is put into planning events to reach out to the community and build up relationships among those who show interest.

Many shepherds find that the transition to developer is difficult. This involves moving beyond their core professional competencies in the traditional church culture. Conflict usually develops with those who value the present culture and sense diminishment of their personal importance and values.

Contrasting Values

Guilt is a powerful motivator in a small established community where people are ready to let their church identity be a firm statement of who they are. Traditionally shepherd ministers can use guilt as an effective motivator for participating in church life. In large sprawling communities of the twenty-first century, however, guilt doesn't work well anymore. Few neighbors know each other. Churchgoers are a minority among the many unchurched around them. The unchurched might respond to an opportunity to fill a personal need, not because of concern of what others will think about them. Developers of ministry become needs oriented.

Where the shepherd would highly value faithfulness to tradition because it has worked so well in the past, the gardener/builder focuses on effectiveness or fruitfulness—what is working now. The shepherd places high value on nurture within the fellowship; the developer is looking for new connections beyond, as well as within, the congregation. Shepherds value uniformity in patterns and practices of church life. Developers bless diversity that better fits the needs and expectations of those with whom they are trying to make new connections.

Contrasting Patterns for Church Life

The pattern of development according to the shepherd model starts with the assumption of belonging; participants are born into the congregation through infant baptism. Then the challenge is to help them learn to believe what the fellowship believes; for children this is done through confirmation. Whether participants have a strong heartfelt experience with God is a low priority; more importantly is living out the shared identity of the flock, the gathered family of God.

Instead of working with the pattern of belonging leading to believing and maybe to experiencing, the church bodies that have been most effective in America follow the opposite pattern: experiencing, believing, and belonging. Such ministry helps participants experience God's presence in their lives, teaches them what to believe about this relationship, and encourages them to become part of the fellowship.

In this nonmainline pattern, being born again into Christian faith is the starting point for a believer, and this has to happen when the individual is old enough to understand the experience and undergo believer baptism. Telling your "born-again story" provides entrance into a church fellowship. The fastest growing expression of Christianity around the world is in Pentecostal forms that stress emotional experiences of the Holy Spirit. Being born of the Spirit is often considered a second spiritual rebirth. Their worship services are usually emotionally charged.

Almost all churches that value their European heritage as an established church body practice infant baptism. In contrast, almost all churches whose heritage is from the American experience practice believer baptism. These two different heritages with their different theologies lead to congregational cultures with differing expectations for the minister. The shepherd is at home in infant-baptizing churches. The developer, to date, is more likely to be found in believer-baptizing congregations. The issue at hand is whether a new breed of developer pastors can find welcome in mainline churches.

Contrasting Perspectives on
Personal Spiritual Experience

A key difference between the shepherd model and developer model is the emphasis on personal experience. The feeding and protecting shepherd in a stable community need not expect that members will have a decisive, memorable personal encounter with God. In fact, anyone acting out a special emotional, very high level of conviction can be unwelcome as disruptive to the many lacking such an experience. This happened in thousands of congregations during the charismatic movement among Episcopalians, Lutherans, and Catholics in the 1960s and '70s.

The planter/gardener/coach/builder welcomes personal subjective experiences and aims to help such experiences happen. They become important connecting points. Key to being drawn to God and a specific congregation is experiencing satisfaction of needs he or she is aware of. In a village, satisfaction and fulfillment aren't important concepts. These are, however, for ministry in suburbs with high turnover and lots of competition.

Such an emphasis on personal spiritual experiences is what perhaps most distinguishes the newer developer model of ministry from the older, traditional shepherd model, which is basic to the mainline heritage of ministry. It also shifts our attention beyond the original shepherd, Jesus, to the original developer of the earliest churches, Paul.

The Differing Emphases of Jesus and Paul

Jesus will always be the Good Shepherd. Psalm 23 ("The Lord Is My Shepherd") will always be the most popular psalm, read at every funeral. It speaks to the one-on-one relationship between Jesus and me—the most fundamental relationship from which everything else in church life flows. In contrast to doctrinal statements favored by churches, this psalm features the feelings associated with my personal shepherd. This fundamental relationship is more a matter of heart than of head.

143

Significantly, in the four Gospel accounts of what Jesus said and did, the sheep/shepherd metaphor appears forty-four times. Jesus referred to "church" only twice.

Paul had a perspective very different from Jesus's. He used the word *shepherd* only once and referred to church sixty times. Certainly he personally experienced a very close relationship to Jesus at his conversion and ever after. But of the two hundred times he referenced Jesus, all but four use his title "Jesus the Christ" or "our Lord Jesus." The exceptions were when he referred to Jesus in his earthly ministry. Paul's one mention of leader as shepherd is significant.[110] He meant it in the sense of those in their fellowship from predators—a high priority today, too.

Jesus, by the power of the Spirit working through him, had the ability to draw followers to him and relate to them in ways that changed their lives. Paul knew he personally didn't have the power to change individual lives, but he observed how the transformation happened again and again through the work of the Spirit. The Spirit appears the most in the Gospel accounts of Luke and John—twenty-eight times with some overlap and mostly as Jesus prepared his disciples for his departure. The Spirit appears in Paul's letters 143 times.

My point for ministry in churches today is that Paul is a better guide, and he didn't make much use of the shepherd metaphor for his work. He was a builder, not a maintainer of what exists.

Here is a summary comparison:

Jesus	Paul
"I am the good shepherd" (John 10:11).	"I am the master builder" (1 Cor. 3:10).
Used sheep/shepherd metaphor forty-four times.	Used shepherd metaphor one time.
Referred to church two times.	Referred to church sixty times.

Used builder metaphor for church one time.

Used builder metaphor twenty-eight times.

Jesus developed personal relationships. Paul developed churches.

Most of what Paul wrote about Jesus Christ is in reference to one side of the coin of God's influence in our daily lives through Jesus Christ. The other side of that coin of God's presence today is the work of the Holy Spirit, the Spirit of Christ. For Paul, having the Spirit in us and Christ in us was one and the same thing. I will repeat here the pairings offered in the Third Discussion.

We are sealed in Christ; we are sealed in the Holy Spirit.

We are consecrated in Christ; we are consecrated in the Holy Spirit.

We are righteous in Christ; we are righteous in the Holy Spirit.

We have life through Christ; we have life through the Spirit.

We have hope grounded in Christ; we have hope grounded in the power of the Spirit.

Christ is the alternative to the law; the Spirit is the alternative to the law.

We are to stand fast in the Lord; we are to stand fast in the one Spirit.

We are to rejoice in the Lord; we have joy in the Holy Spirit.

We are told to live in Christ; we are told to walk in the Spirit.

Paul spoke the truth in Christ; Paul spoke the truth in the Spirit.

We are called into the fellowship of Christ; we are blessed with the fellowship of the Holy Spirit.

My point with the two sides of the same coin is that mainline churches today would do well to shift their attention to the other side, the Christ's Spirit side. Such emphasis isn't our heritage. Our churches are withering. Yet the church of Christ today is flourishing among Christ's followers who emphasize the Holy Spirit. With theological and rational integrity, we can learn from Paul how to better cultivate the work of the Spirit in our churches.

Jesus, my personal Savior, will always be basic to the Christian message and mission. But from the very beginning, the message and mission have been carried on by groupings of followers. These would be house churches at Paul's time and are now congregations of whatever size. When it comes to forming and leading Christian congregations in our times, Paul and his very early churches provide the best model for church leadership today.

Over the centuries Christian churches, under the influence of the Spirit, have adapted to changing social and political circumstances around them. For two thousand years those structures have taken many different forms and adapted different approaches to ministry, sometimes with very tight organization, other times with more fluid forms. Early twenty-first-century Christians in North America face a major change in both social and political circumstances. Many may want to shake their heads and complain about loss of respect for the old church ways. What's much more productive is to adapt and get on with the developer's focus on the benefits of following Jesus, as produced by his Spirit.

Discussion Questions

1. What are your feelings about a pastor serving as a shepherd?
2. How do you react to the thought of a pastor as a developer who plants seeds, does gardening, coaches growth, and builds up the fellowship?
3. Do any of you have experiences of living in a small town? How is such a small town different from the suburbs today? How would you describe the gentle pressure toward conformity?
4. What do you think of the contrast between infant-baptizing churches and believer-baptizing churches?
5. How do you react to the contrast between the emphases of Jesus and Paul?

Afterword
This Theology of God the Third Person

Envision the Christ figure in Revelation 3:20, who is knocking at the door. For us now this is Christ's Spirit, who wants us to open the door so he can come in and be with us. He does this daily and even many times a day. Our challenge is to learn to recognize him at the door of our thoughts and respond in the conversation called prayer.

This view differs from classical Protestant theology of the Reformation, in which the Holy Spirit is left vaguely in the background. We have inherited a binitarian emphasis on God the Father and God the Son. Reemphasizing God the Spirit, who proceeds from the Father and the Son, can restore a full biblical Trinitarian theology for ministry today.

Christ's Spirit is one of twenty-four different names for the Spirit in the New Testament alone. I'm focusing on Paul's theology of the Spirit, especially because of his emphasis on gifts and fruit of the Spirit. Formative for me was Gordon D. Fee's major study of *God's Empowering Presence: The Holy Spirit in Paul's Letters.* He observes,

> The Spirit of God is also the Spirit of Christ, who carries on the work of Christ following his resurrection and subsequent assumption of the place of authority at God's right hand. To have received the Spirit of God is to have the mind of Christ. For Paul, therefore, Christ gives definition to the Spirit. Thus it is fair to say that Paul's doctrine of the Spirit is Christocentric in the sense that Christ and his work give definition to the Spirit and his work in the Christian life.[111]

Jesus himself declares that "the Father will give you another Counselor, the Spirit of truth, who will live with you and be in you. This Counselor, the Holy Spirit, whom the Father will send in my name, will teach you all things and remind you of everything I have said."[112]

A breakthrough insight for me was systematic theologian Lewis Smedes's arrangement of eleven parallel passages that attribute the same characteristic to Christ in one place and to the Spirit in another. (as listed in Chapter 1 and on page 137; See endnote 36 for the citations.) Life in Christ is the same as life in the Holy Spirit.

Spirit from Christ

Another breakthrough came with the realization that "the Holy Spirit" isn't really a title for the third person of the Trinity, even though "Holy" is the description consistently used in confessional and doctrinal statements. Gordon Fee recognizes 143 references to the Spirit in Paul's writing. In only seventeen did Paul name him the "Holy Spirit." Sixteen times he referred to "God's Spirit." Seven times he named the Spirit of Christ, the Lord, the Son of God. John's Gospel gives us the fullest description of the relationship between Jesus Christ and the Spirit. In thirteen references to the Spirit, Jesus and John the Baptist named him the Holy Spirit only three times.

Why, then, do we continue to refer to the third person of the Trinity as the Holy Spirit? New Testament writers undoubtedly carried forward the heavy Old Testament use of "holy" as the description for God and his special places, such as the holy of holies, where God was especially present in the temple. When the early Christian church councils were working out the relationships of the three-in-one God, they needed to distinguish the third person, separate from the Father and the Son. Using "holy" as a title for the Spirit helped.

Fully respecting the mystery of the Trinity, I propose that "Christ's Spirit" is a better descriptor for the Spirit, as the apostle Paul knew and explained. His emphasis on grace, made possible through the redemptive work of Christ, is basic to the Protestant interpretation of the New Testament. Jesus the Christ's human birth, life, death, and resurrection happened in biblical times twenty centuries ago. He continues with us today through his Spirit.

Jesus himself clarified this relationship when he told his followers, "All that belongs to the Father is mine. That is why I said the Spirit will take from what is mine and make it known to you."[113]

The second-century Apostles Creed tidies up the logic by confessing that "Jesus ascended into heaven and sits on the right hand of the Father, and He shall come again with glory to judge both the living and the dead." After his ascension on the fortieth day after Easter and before he returns in the final judgment, Christ is in heaven in a position of authority with his Father and thus is present among his followers through his Spirit.

The "Spirit *from* Christ" clarifies the relationship best of all. It certainly fits the fourth-century Nicene Creed's explanation that "we believe in the Holy Spirit, the Lord and Giver of Life, who proceeds from the Father and the Son." In Greek grammar this name is related to the noun Spirit in genitive form, which can be either the genitive of possession, "Spirit of Christ," or the genitive of source, "Spirit from Christ." Hear "Christ's Spirit" in the genitive form of the Spirit from Christ.

Those who know their history of Christian doctrine can point to the "filioque" controversy about whether the Spirit proceeds only from the Father, as Eastern Orthodoxy confesses, or also from the Father and the Son, as the Western Catholic tradition believes. Descended from that tradition, Protestants believe "filioque," that the Spirit proceeds from the Father "and the Son." But English style is served best by shortening the five syllables in "the Spirit from Christ" to the three in "Christ's Spirit."

How Important Are the Spiritual Gifts?

Strangely overlooked from the earliest centuries on is Paul's distinctive emphasis on the gifts of the Spirit or spiritual gifts. Reflective of that approach is a 1960s publication on the *Half-Known God* in my church body.[114] The gifts of the Spirit received just one paragraph of attention in passing. The fruit of the Spirit got the same one-paragraph treatment.

Initially set forth in 1 Corinthians 12, Paul condensed his description of the gifts several years later in Romans 12. Yet another few years later, he gave an echo of this teaching in Ephesians 4. There he had the short list of those given to be apostles, prophets, evangelists, pastors, and teachers. By the time the Christian church was heavily institutionalized in the fourth century, these functions had become offices, and these offices were grouped together as clergy, and the clergy were inclined to think of themselves as God's gift to the laity—everyone else. They became the keepers of the Spirit. This interpretation continued well into the twentieth century in the mainline churches of the Reformation. The book of doctrine I learned from has the conventional first volume on the Father and the second on the Son. But the third starts with the church and its pastoral office. There is not even one chapter the God the Spirit.[115]

What put spiritual gifts back on the agenda of Protestant churches is the Pentecostal movement, especially as it become more widely accepted in the latter part of the twentieth century. What set them apart is their celebration of the Spirit, manifesting himself through the gifts of speaking in tongues and also miraculous healings. These are presented in Paul's 1 Corinthians 12 account of the spiritual gifts, although they are no longer in his Romans 12 listing.

This focus on several spiritual gifts naturally led to consideration of the others. Spiritual gift inventories were beginning to appear in the 1980s. Their usefulness for organizing the work of a congregation became readily apparent. Too often, though, these questionnaires were used without much attention to the special motivation by the Spirit that Paul assumed.

Paul's understanding of the gifts of the Spirit, as given to all who confess Christ, was radical at his time. A prevailing notion was that the Spirit was something given only to a favored few, and many in the Corinthian congregation doubted that Paul was among them. The full range of gifts of the Spirit is radical in the mainline Protestant churches today and brings with it a reconsideration of the distinction between clergy and laity.

It is also reshaping how believers are called and prepared for ministries of the word. Four years of college and three years of seminary need not be the only route. Indeed this traditional mainline church approach may not even be the best in comparison to course work accompanying hands-on experience of those the church recognizes as called for leadership in ministry. Giftedness for ministry isn't necessarily the same as giftedness for seven years of post-secondary academic success.

The gifts of the Spirit also invite new perspective on the fruit of the Spirit, which Paul treats as a subset of spiritual gifts—the greater gifts.[116] In the workshops I do, many are able to recite with me Paul's listing in Galatians 5:22: "love, joy, peace, patience, kindness, goodness, faithfulness, gentleness, and self-control." But what are these fruit? It is fruit singular, because the Greek can best be translated as product. These are the product of the Spirit's work.

Traditionally they are called virtues. In the preceding chapters I have treated them as feelings. Use of this simple, well-known word challenges some basic assumptions in Reformation theology. Are love, joy, peace, and the other fruit good works and therefore involved in the sanctification process? As such they can be seen as the product of rational decisions and thus considered matters of the head. Jesus himself explained to Nicodemus that the "Spirit influences human spirit (John 3:6)." The hearts of believers become different through the Spirit's work in them. Such Spirit-influenced hearts yield more Christ-like behaviors. The Spirit is the key to the sanctification process. Or are they inner predispositions and thus matters of the heart? What is the relationship between head and heart in a believer's relationship to God.

Spirit-given Motivation for Sanctification

Central to the Reformation confrontation with Catholicism was the role of good works. That discussion was carried on through the distinction between justification (being made just before God) and sanctification (being made holy and doing good works). The Protestant position was and is that we are saved by God's grace, not by our works. In my Lutheran heritage we have been hesitant to preach about sanctification lest human behaviors be confused with God's freely given justification.

But that centuries-long discussion and concern is shifting—not in the direction of more emphasis on how to behave, but toward even greater emphasis on God's grace and gifts. For centuries of Reformation scholarship, forensic justification by grace through faith was considered central to Paul's theology. Current biblical scholarship emphasizes also the faith not just declared but actually experienced, and many scholars now conclude that "Paul's doctrine of the Spirit is far more central and characteristic than his doctrine of justification by faith."[117]

The Reformation was all about accepting that justification is God's work based on the redemption earned by Jesus Christ. It is given freely. The tendency with sanctification is to see it as something we humans do through focusing on virtuous behavior. But for Paul sanctification, too, is God's work accomplished through Christ's Spirit.

He rejoiced that believers have sanctified status (through justification), and he liked to call the members of churches "the holy ones," the saints. He focused specifically on the process of being made holy only twelve times,[118] and clearly it was the work of the Spirit .[119] More important are the hundreds of references he made to the product of the Spirit's work in a believer like, but not limited to, the nine fruit of love, joy, peace, patience, kindness, goodness, faithfulness, gentleness, and self-control. Add thanksgiving and hope. These were inner pre-dispositions of mind and heart—feelings influenced by the Spirit—that motivate more God-pleasing behaviors. Sanctified behaviors weren't self-generated in response to commandments demanding good works. They were Spirit-generated within and resulted outwardly in God-pleasing behaviors.

Paul did not give commandments to those gathered in Christ's name. He reminded them of their new motivation through Christ's Spirit and then encouraged them to work out the specific applications in situations they encountered. While he set expectations for our new nature in Christ, He was aware that our old sinful nature always remains with us in this world. It is the Spirit's work to turn old natures into new Christ-centered lives characterized by ever deeper love, joy and peace. The result of his work is our changed behavior.

Hearts as Well as Heads

Before explaining why inner dispositions, "feelings," is the best description, I need to highlight another major assumption in Christian theology from the earliest centuries up to the twentieth. Reason was much more important than emotions. Said another way, emotions were very suspect as a basis for guiding behavior. This perspective is built into the Western intellectual tradition, epitomized by the Stoics. Centuries of theologians cautioned against is what we could call "raw emotions," such as fear, jealousy, or hatred. Basically, think before you act, especially when it comes to God's will in your life. Stick to the well-reasoned word.

In ways that seem almost naïve now, the reasoning of heads was assumed to be the key to shaping right behavior. In medieval education and through centuries since the Reformation, the "trivium" was considered fundamental to education of youth. This encompassed the three subjects of logic, grammar, and rhetoric. Rhetoric was the art of persuading audiences, based on proper logic and grammar. The underlying assumption was that if something could just be explained well enough, the hearers would understand and do accordingly. Hence we have the catechisms used by historic Protestant as well as Roman Catholic church bodies

In this context love was approached as a rational attraction to someone or something. We know today that love involves much more in determining behavior. In fact, the symbol of the red *heart* is universally recognized now as communicating love. In earlier times, there was no framework for understanding matters of the heart in any depth.

Today we know much more about motivation, the subject of my academic specialty of organization behavior. It is something that arises from within persons and puts them into motion to satisfy a perceived need. Coaches cannot motivate players, but they can arrange a sequence of experiences that will enable a player to rise to a peak performance that best satisfies his or her inner drive. Motivation is all about emotions. The word *emotions* itself means to put into motion, which is fundamental to motivation.

New Testament scholar Matthew Elliott has rescued emotions from their low status in Christian thought. He labels Paul's fruit of the Spirit—such as love, joy, and peace—as *Faithful Feelings,* the title of his book.[120] He offers the helpful distinction between age-old *somatic* theory of emotions based on reactions manifested bodily, as in the flushed look of anger or the jittery legs of impatience. Today the whole counseling enterprise works rather on *cognitive*, brain-based theories for how a person's emotions can change by altering his or her perception of the cause for his or her dysfunctional emotional reaction.

Modern English doesn't lend itself well to naming the fundamental inner predisposition described today as feelings, emotions, or spirit. *Affections* would be the best, as American theologian Jonathan Edwards defined it several centuries ago. For him these were strong inclinations manifested in thinking, feeling, and acting.[121] But the word *affections* doesn't communicate well anymore. The word *feelings* does the best job in modern English.

The Spirit and Matters of the Heart

Motivation is an inner predisposition to do something. Feelings are inner affections. Both arise from within. Paul prayed that the Father may "strengthen you with power through his Spirit in your inner being, so that Christ may dwell in your hearts through faith.[122] The "within" is what he and we call the heart—subject to, but not limited to, normal reasoning. Paul gave us the wonderful image of seeing with the eyes of the heart.[123] Such seeing is to be fully enlightened in greater depth to experience love beyond reason.

For the highly educated Reformers in an age of superstition and widespread illiterate ignorance, reason was the key to the better Christian life. For them there was no great need to depend on the Spirit to change hearts. Shaping head knowledge accomplished a lot.

Today we know much more about the limits of words and reason. Even the best counselors admit that changing inner perceptions is slow and usually not profound. Rather than reason, the key to changing hearts is experiences.

Offering and interpreting experiences of God's love and Christ's grace are the fundamental challenge of ministry. That challenge is even greater for those of us who minister out of the Reformers' heritage of strong bias against recognizing emotional experiences.

Paul knew better than to rely on normal head knowledge. For him the key to eyes of the heart in relation to God was the Holy Spirit. May the Father "give you the Spirit of wisdom and revelation so you may know him better. I pray also that the eyes of your heart may be enlightened."[124]

What the Spirit does best is expressed in Paul's use of the word *transformed*. "We are being transformed into (Christ's) likeness with ever-increasing glory, which comes from the Lord who is the Spirit." He wrote to the Romans that we are to be transformed through the renewing of our minds, no longer conforming to the patterns of this world.[125] Like the word *fellowship*, the word *transformed* has been trivialized in modern English, becoming almost any kind of minor change. The word in Greek gives us metamorphosis, the complete change that happens when a caterpillar becomes a butterfly.

Rather than leaving the Holy Spirit vaguely in the background, we need to bring him to the foreground as the ascended Spirit from Christ, who is the active agent in changing hearts of believers here and now.

How did mainline churches go for centuries without explicitly recognizing the work of the Spirit in their midst? They were privileged in the politics of their home countries. Not to be a Christian was unthinkable and brought heavy penalties. The political sociology confined arguments to points of doctrine on how to be saved.

Today in the mainline homelands, churched Christians are becoming the minority. The majority don't worry about eternal destiny and no longer recognize the scriptures as a God-inspired source of authority. They are inclined to judge Christianity on the basis of its impact on the daily lives of believers. Our best witness is to reflect lives characterized by love, joy, peace, patience, and the other products of the Spirit's work.

Saved by Grace to Live by Grace

Thank God he gave his people inspired scriptures that present theology for basing our witness on the quality of life in this world in addition to the next, as developed previously in Discussion 4. Jesus was all about expanding God's kingdom, which yields the abundant life he came to give his followers. Paul highlighted the gifts of the Spirit that change our inner being to produce new motivations and more life-affirming feelings.

Paul's theology addressed two different audiences. He started with the Jews in mind, his own people, out of whom came the Messiah. To them he stressed salvation by grace through faith, not by works obedient to the law. That the Messiah arrived in the person of the rabbi Jesus was a powerful argument among Jews, and we have glimpses of Paul as he reasoned with Jews in synagogues when he first arrived in a new city.

The other audience was everybody else, the Gentiles. Reaching them was much more difficult because they had no expectation of a God-promised Messiah. There was little common ground for reasoning. Paul was utterly dependent on the Spirit to change them into loving and joyful believers. Experiencing the difference was much more important for reaching Gentiles. So was dependence on the Spirit to produce those changes.

In his writings Paul carefully distinguished between the grace given, *charis*, and grace received, *charisma*. The grace given is God's pronouncement of righteousness in Christ. The grace received is experiences of the Spirit working changes within a believer's motivation and feeling. These permit moving beyond salvation by grace to daily living by grace.

For most of its history, the Christian church could assume Christian faith and identity among those to whom it ministered. With such common ground, reason could prevail.

That common ground of identity is disappearing in Europe and North America. In response, churches faithful to their mission need to elevate the importance of experiences of God today. To do that the work of the Spirit needs to be moved into the foreground of witness today.

The importance of experiencing Christ's Spirit becomes apparent through simple reasoning with numbers. As noted several times earlier in this book, Christianity is growing in the world faster now than at any other time in its history. Almost all of that growth is in Pentecostal and charismatic expressions. By definition such churches share experiences of the Spirit.

All Christians need to be cautious that the spirit they are experiencing is the Spirit who proceeds from the Father and the Son, as presented in the word. The key characteristic of a life changed by the Spirit is a new kind of convicted knowing and genuine humility.[126] In addition, church bodies that emphasize careful reasoning will always be cautious of irrational experiences. But as I have tried to show, there are plenty of ways to experience the Spirit from Christ that are subject to reason and do indeed glorify the ascended Christ.

This afterword on "The Theology of Christ's Spirit" summarizes the biblical truths presented in this book. The

David S. Luecke

first half emphasized naming and sharing encounters with the Spirit. The second half was about deliberately seeking more such experiences. Conventionally one would start with the theory (theology) and then move to application. Communication, however, is much more effective when presenting the application and then moving to the underlying theory that gives coherence.

Referring to Christ's Spirit is one way to distinguish this milder version from the Holy Spirit the Pentecostals emphasize.

Traditional Protestant churches don't need to continue withering away. Thriving in Christ's Spirit is something for which we can pray and prepare ourselves.

Endnotes

1   The New Testament alone has twenty names for the Spirit. Of the 143 relevant passages in Paul's writings, Gordon Fee cites (*God's Empowering Presence*, 1995) by far the most simple name, "the Spirit." Only seventeen name "the Holy Spirit." "Spirit of God"/"His Spirit" occurs sixteen times. "Spirit of Christ"/"Lord"/"Son of God" occurs seven times: Rom. 1:4; 8:9; Gal. 4:6; Eph. 3:17; Phil. 1:19; and 2 Cor. 3:17–18. Peter named the Spirit of Christ: 1 Peter 1:11. Hebrews names the Spirit of grace: 10:29.

    In Greek grammar the genitive of the "Spirit *of* Christ" and the "Spirit *of* God" can also be properly called the "Spirit *from* Christ" and the "Spirit *from* God."

2   Ephesians 3:16–17.
3   Romans 5:5.
4   Romans 1:4.
5   Romans 2:4.
6   John 10:10.
7   John 15:11.
8   John 17:13.
9   Luke 15:11.
10 Luke 15:23.
11 Gordon D. Fee, *God's Empowering Presence*, (Hendrickson Publishers 1995), 1.
12 Allen Anderson, *Studying Global Pentecostalism* (University of California Press, 2010).
13 Greg L. Hawkins and Cally Parkinson, *Move: What 1,000 Churches REVEAL about Spiritual Growth* (Grand Rapids, MI: Zondervan, 2011), 266.

Chapter 2
14 Matthew 11:28–30.
15 Luke 9:23–24.
16 Romans 8:2.
17 2 Corinthians 3:7.
18 2 Corinthians 3:18.
19 Ephesians 1:18.

20 John 7:38.
21 John Ortberg, *The Me I Want to Be*, (Grand Rapids, Zondervan, 2010) 43. Other references are on 23, 34, 39, 49, 52.
22 John Eldridge and Brent Curtis, *The Sacred Romance* (Nashville, Thomas Nelson, 1997) 2, 9, 19, 31, 42, 91.
23 Matthew 16:25 (MSG).
24 Dallas Willard, *Renovation of the Heart* (NavPress, 2002) 23.
25 Dallas Willard, *The Divine Conspiracy* (San Francisco, Harper Collins, 1998), 350.
26 John Koenig, *Charismata: God's Gifts for God's People* (1978), 122.
27 Fee, *God's Empowering Presence*, 1.
28 David S. Luecke, *Your Encounters with the Holy Spirit* (Bloomington IN, Westbow Press, 2014), 16.

Chapter 3
30 Matthew 3: 17.
31 John 14: 15, 16, 26.
32 John 16: 7, 15.
33 Galatians 5:22.
34 Romans 12:6–8.
35 Luecke, *Your Encounters*, 78–81.
36 We are sealed in Christ (Eph. 1:13).
    We are sealed in the Holy Spirit (Eph. 1:13).
    We are consecrated in Christ (1 Cor. 1:3).
    We are consecrated in the Holy Spirit (Rom. 12:15:15).
    We are righteous in Christ (Phil. 3:8–9).
    We are righteous in the Holy Spirit (Rom. 14:17).
    We are righteous in both (1 Cor. 6:11).
    We have life through Christ (Eph. 2:11; Col. 3:4).
    We have life through the Holy Spirit (Rom. 8:11).
    We have hope grounded in Christ (1 Cor. 15:9).
    We have hope grounded in the power of the Holy Spirit (Gal. 6:8).
    Christ is the alternative. The Spirit is the alternative to the law of sin and death (Rom. 8:2).
    We are commanded to stand fast in the Lord (Phil. 4:1).
    We are told to stand fast in the one Spirit (Phil. 1:27).
    We are told to rejoice in the Lord (Phil. 4:4).
    We are told to have joy in the Holy Spirit (Rom. 14:17).

We are told to live in Christ (Col. 2:6).

We are told to walk in the Holy Spirit (Eph. 4:3; Gal. 5:25).

Paul speaks the truth in the Christ (Rom. 9:11; 2 Cor. 2:17).

Paul speaks the truth in the Holy Spirit (1 Cor. 12:3).

We are called into the fellowship of Christ (1 Cor. 1:9).

We are blessed with the fellowship of the Holy Spirit (2 Cor. 13:14).

36 Kohlenberger, Goodrick, and Swanson, *The Exhaustive Concordance to the Greek New Testament* (Grand Rapids, Zondervan,1995), 1008

37 Fee, *God's Empowering Presence*, Passages listed in Table of Contents.

38 Lewis B. Smedes, *Union with Christ* (Grand Rapids, Eerdmans,1983), 54.

39 Ephesians 1:7.

40 James E. Loder, *The Transforming Moment*, 2nd ed. (1989), 10, 19, 22–24.

41 Gideon Lichfield, "Solving the Riddle of Near-Death Experiences," *Atlantic Monthly*, April 2015, 76.

42 1 John 4: 1-4.

Chapter 4

43 Romans 8:23.

44 John 10:10.

45 Titus 3:5.

46 Romans 15:13.

47 Romans 14:17.

48 John 3:16.

49 Fee, *God's Empowering Presence*, 84.

50 Ibid., 869.

51 Luke 11:13.

52 Romans 14:17.

53 Ephesians 3:16.

54 Mark 4:26–28.

55 Matthew 13:1–9.

56 1 Corinthians 3:6–7.

57 Ephesians 4:12.

Chapter 6

58 2 Peter 3:18.

59 Romans 5:6.

60 Romans 12:6.
61 Koenig, *Charismata*, 49.
62 1 Corinthians 3:6.
63 Philippians 1:25–26.
64 1 Thessalonians 3:12.
65 2 Thessalonians 1:3.
66 Philippians 1:9.
67 1 Thessalonians 1:6.
68 Colossians 1:6.
69 Romans 14:17.
70 Romans 15:13.
71 2 Corinthians 8:1.
72 Ephesians 2:9
73 Sanctification as process: Romans 6:22 and 1 Thessalonians 4:7; 5:23. Sanctification as the work of the Holy Spirit: Romans 15:16 and 2 Thessalonians 2:13.
74 Colossians 2:6–7.

Chapter 7
75 Galatians 5:25.
76 Gary Thomas, *Sacred Pathways* (Thomas Nelson, 1996), 270.
77 John Koenig, *Charismata*, 122.
78 James Fowler, *Stages of Faith: The Psychology of Human Development and the Quest for Meaning* (1995). The names for these stages are from Thomas Droege, *Faith Passages and Patterns* (Philadelphia, Fortress Press, 1983).
79 *Luther's Works*, vol. 44 (Fortress, 1966), 240–243.
80 Romans 8:19.
81 Galatians 4:19.
82 Philippians 2:5–6.
83 Ephesians 4:13.
84 Greg L. Hawkins and Cally Parkinson, *Move: What 1,000 Churches Reveal about Spiritual Growth* (Grand Rapids, Zondervan, 2011), 193–250.
85 2 Corinthians 3:17.

Chapter 8
86 Richard Foster, *Celebration of Discipline: Path to Spiritual Growth* (HarperCollins, 1978), 6.

87   Nathan Foster, *The Making of an Ordinary Saint* (Baker Books, 2014), 8.

88   Luke 11: 13.

89   Adolf Koeberle, *The Quest for Holiness* (Augsburg, 1938), 175.

90   Donald G Bloesch, *The Struggle of Prayer* (Helmers and Howard, 1988), 60.

91   Matthew 19:23.

92   Luke 9:23.

93   Henry T. Blackaby and Claude King, *Experiencing God* (Nashville, B and H Publishing Group, 1990).

Chapter 9

94   Charles J. Keating, *Who We Are Is How We Pray* (Mystic Connecticut, Twenty Third Publications, 1987.)

95   Gary Thompson, *Sacred Pathways to God; Discover your Soul's Path to God* (Grand Rapids, Zondervan, 1996).

96   Ann and Barry Ulanov, *Primary Speech: A Psychology of Prayer* (Atlanta, John Knox Press, 1982), 20.

97   1 Corinthians 3:10.

Chapter 10

98   1 Corinthians 10: 16

99   1 John 1: 3

100 1 Corinthians 12: 12-26, Ephesians 4: 12

101 Ephesians 2: 19-22

102 1 Corinthians 3: 9-10

103 Ephesians 4: 12-13

104 1 Corinthians 3: 6

105 1 Corinthians 1:9; 2 Corinthians 13: 14, Philippians 2: 1

106 1 Corinthians 14: 5, 17; 8: 1; 10:23; Romans 15: 19; 15:2; Ephesians 4: 29

107 Luke 11:13

108 David S. Luecke, *Builder Ministry in the 21st Century* (St. Louis, CPH, 2010).

109 David S. Luecke, *Your Encounters with the Holy Spirit: Name and Share Them—Seek More*, (Bloomington, Westbow Press, 2010).

Chapter 11

110 Acts 20: 28

Afterword

111 Fee, *God's Empowering Presence*, 837.

112 John 14:17, 26.

113 John 16:15.

114 Lorenz Wunderlich, *The Half-Known God* (Concordia Publishing House, 1963).

115 Francis Pieper, *Christian Dogmatics*, (St. Louis, Concordia Publishing House, 1950)

116 1 Corinthians 12: 31

117 S. Neill and N. T. Wright, *The Interpretation of the New Testament 1861-1986* (Oxford Press, 1988) 203, as cited in Gordon E. Fee, 1.

118 Romans 6:19, 22; 12:1; 15:16; 1 Corinthians 1:2; Ephesians 5:26; 1 Thessalonians 4:3–4, 7; 5:23; 2 Thessalonians 2:13; 1 Timothy 4:5.

119 Romans 15:16; 2 Thessalonians 2:13.

120 Matthew Elliott, *Faithful Feelings: Rethinking Emotions in the New Testament* (2006).

121 Luecke, *Your Encounters*, 22

122 Ephesians 3:16–17.

123 Ephesians 1:18.

124 Ephesians 1: 17, 18.

125 2 Corinthians 3:18; Romans 12:1.

126 Luecke, *Your Encounters*, 23

CPSIA information can be obtained
at www.ICGtesting.com
Printed in the USA
LVOW12s1245050417
529621LV00001B/1/P